Mammals of the San Gabriel Mountains of California

by Terry A. Vaughan

CONTENTS

INTRODUCTION

This paper presents the results of a study of the mammals of the San Gabriel Mountains of southern California, and supplements the more extensive reports on the biota of the San Bernardino Mountains by Grinnell (1908), on the fauna of the San Jacinto Range by Grinnell and Swarth (1913), and on the biota of the Santa Ana Mountains by Pequegnat (1951).

The primary objectives of my study were to determine the present mammalian fauna of the San Gabriel Mountains, to ascertain the geographic and ecologic range of each species, and to determine the systematic status of the mammals. In addition, certain life history observations have been recorded.

Field work was done in the north-south cross section of the mountains from San Gabriel Canyon on the west, to Cajon Wash on the east; and from the gently sloping alluvium at the Pacific base of the mountains at roughly 1000 feet elevation on the south, over the crest of the range to the border of the Mojave Desert at an elevation of 3500 feet on the north. Camps were established at many points in the area with the object of collecting the mammals of each association and each habitat. Field work was begun in the San Gabriels in November 1948, and was carried on intermittently until March

1952. I was unable to carry on field work in any summer.

For advice and assistance in various ways I am grateful to Drs. Willis E. Pequegnat, Walter P. Taylor, Henry S. Fitch, E. Raymond Hall, Mr. Steven M. Jacobs and my wife, Hazel A. Vaughan.

More than 350 mammals were prepared as study specimens; most of these are in the University of Kansas Museum of Natural History. Approximately a fifth of them are in the collection of the Department of Zoology at Pomona College, and a few are in the University of Illinois Museum of Natural History. No symbol is used to designate specimens in the University of Kansas Museum of Natural History. Specimens from the Department of Zoology of Pomona College and the University of Illinois Museum of Natural History are designated by PC and IM, respectively.

DESCRIPTION OF THE AREA

The San Gabriel Mountains are approximately sixty-six miles long, and average twenty miles wide. The main axis of the range trends nearly east and west, and extends from longitude 117 deg.25' to longitude 118 deg.30'. The widest part of the range is bounded by latitude 34 deg.7' and latitude 34 deg.30'.

The San Gabriel Mountains connect the Sierra Nevada with the Peninsular Ranges of southern California and Baja California. On the west the San Gabriels are bordered by the Tehachapi Mountains, which stretch northeastward to meet the southern Sierra Nevada; to the east, beyond Cajon Pass, the San Bernardino Mountains extend eastward and then curve southward to the broad San Gorgonio Pass, from which the San Jacinto Range stretches southeastward to merge with the Peninsular Ranges.

The rocks comprising the major part of the San Gabriel Mountains probably were intruded in Late Jurassic times, with severe metamorphic activity taking place concurrently. A long period of erosion followed after which deposition took place during much of the Tertiary. Deformation and uplift beginning in Middle Miocene times resulted in the formation of east-west-trending faults along both sides of the range. By repeated movements along these faults the Late Jurassic crystalline rocks were lifted above late Tertiary and Quaternary sediments and elevated above the surrounding terrain. Continued uplifts in post-Pleistocene time together with erosion in Recent times have shaped the San Gabriel Mountains (Oakeshott, 1937).

The alluvial slopes at the coastal base of the range give way to the foothills at roughly 1800 feet elevation; whereas the Mojave Desert merges with the interior foothills at elevations near 4000 feet. The crest or drainage-divide of the range varies from 6000 to 8000 feet in elevation, and many peaks are more than 8000 feet high. San Antonio Peak, the highest peak of the range, rises to an altitude of 10,080 feet. The mountains are characteristically steep and the slopes are deeply carved by canyons, the larger of which have permanent streams. The abruptness of the Pacific slope is in many places impressive. The horizontal distance from the top of Cucamonga Peak, at an elevation of 8911 feet, to the base of the coastal foothills directly to the south, at 2250 feet, an elevational difference of 6661 feet, is only 3.8 miles. From the base of Evey Canyon, at 2250 feet, to an unnamed peak to the northwest with an elevation of 5420 feet, the horizontal distance is 2.1 miles. Because of the steep, rocky nature of many of the slopes and the lack of soil on them, vegetation may be sparse even at high elevations. There are few meadows in the mountains.

Because the San Gabriels stand approximately thirty miles from the Pacific Ocean and are a partial barrier to Pacific air masses sweeping inland, the desert side and the coastal side of the range differ climatically. The coastal slope receives much heavier precipitation than the desert slope. The precipitation, for 1951, of 25.36 inches recorded at the mouth of San Antonio Canyon on the Pacific slope contrasts with 7.17 inches recorded at Valyermo at the desert base. Nearly all of the precipitation comes in winter. The higher parts of the range, above approximately 5000 feet, receive much of their mid-winter precipitation in the form of snow. Snow often extends down the desert slope well into the Joshua Tree belt. When there are heavy winter rains the channels of the usually dry washes are filled with rushing, turbid water. There are striking differences in temperature between the two sides of the range and between the lower elevations of the mountains and the higher parts. For example, in December 1951, the mean temperature at the base of San Antonio Canyon (2225 feet) at the coastal foot of the range was 55.4 deg.F, while at Llano (3764 feet) at the desert base it was 43.7 deg.F. In this same year the December mean for Table Mountain (7500 feet), on the desert slope, was 33.4 deg.F. The temperature means for July, 1951, at San Antonio Canyon, Llano, and Table Mountain, were 77.3 deg.F, 82.1 deg.F, and 69.2 deg.F respectively. The weather records for 1951 were used for illustration because average temperature and average precipitation for many other years are lacking for most of the weather stations in the area. There is an important difference in the humidity on the two sides of the range, but actual data are not available. At certain times, especially in spring, fog banks moving in from the Pacific Ocean frequently blanket the coastal base of the mountains and the foothills. On such days the fog generally "burns off" in the morning, but may persist into the afternoon or throughout the day. Never in my experience has fog spilled over the main part of the range far onto the desert slope, although the fog may push through the lower passes to be dissipated quickly in the dry desert atmosphere. The obvious differences in the biota on the two sides of the range are probably due to the contrasting climates.

BIOTIC PROVINCES AND ECOLOGIC ASSOCIATIONS

Because of the elevational extremes and attendant climatic contrasts in the San Gabriel Mountains, there is a rather wide range of environmental conditions. Four life-zones are represented: Lower Sonoran, Upper Sonoran, Transition, and Canadian. Within these zones certain ecologic communities can be recognized; these represent several biotic provinces. Table 1 shows the relationships between the environmental categories recognized by the writer in the San Gabriel Mountains. The biotic province and ecologic community system is that developed by Munz and Keck (1949), and the life-zone system is that of Merriam (1898).

TABLE 1.--RELATIONS OF THE MAJOR ENVIRONMENTAL CATEGORIES OF THE SAN GABRIEL MOUNTAINS.

Biotic province	Plant community	Life-zone	Slope
Californian	1. Coastal sage scrub	Lower Sonoran	Pacific
	2. Southern oak woodland	Upper Sonoran	Pacific
	3. Chaparral	Upper Sonoran	Pacific
Sierran	4. Yellow pine forest and limited areas of Canadian and boreal flora	Transition and boreal	Pacific and Desert
Nevadan	5. Sagebrush scrub	Transition Upper Sonoran	Desert
Southern Desert	6. Pinyon-juniper woodland	Upper Sonoran	Desert
	7. Joshua tree woodland	Lower Sonoran	Desert

The Californian Biotic Province dominates the biotic aspect of the coastal slope of the range. Thirty-nine out of the seventy-two mammals recorded from the San Gabriels are typical of this Province. The coastal sage-flats at the Pacific base of the mountains and the vast tracts of chaparral of the coastal slope are included in this Province.

Forming a hiatus between the Pacific and the desert slope is the Sierran Biotic Province consisting of coniferous forests on the crest of the range. The chipmunk (Eutamias speciosus speciosus) and the introduced black bear (Ursus americanus californiensis) are the only two mammals which can be considered typical of this area. On the higher peaks of the range, such as Mount San Antonio and Mount Baden Powell, the Canadian Life-zone is represented by certain boreal plants.

At scattered points along the crest of the range and on the desert slope, the Nevadan Biotic Province is represented by the sagebrush scrub association. No mammals can be considered typical of this region.

The Southern Desert Biotic Province occurs below 6000 feet elevation on the interior slope of the range, and markedly influences the mammal fauna of this slope. Twenty-one species of mammals are typical of this Province.

SCIENTIFIC AND COMMON NAMES OF PLANTS MENTIONED IN THIS REPORT

Pinus lambertiana Sugar Pine P. monophylla One-leaf Pinyon P. ponderosa Yellow Pine P. contorta Lodge-pole Pine Pseudotsuga macrocarpa Big-cone Spruce Abies concolor White Fir Libocedrus decurrens Incense-Cedar Juniperus californica Juniper Ephedra sp. Desert-Tea Bromus sp. Brome Grass Yucca Whipplei Spanish Bayonet Y. brevifolia Joshua Tree Salix sp. Willow Alnus rhombifolia Alder Castanopsis sempervirens Chinquapin Quercus Kelloggii California Black Oak Q. agrifolia California Live Oak Q. dumosa Scrub Oak Eriogonum fasciculatum California Buckwheat Umbellularia californica Bay, California-laurel Ribes nevadense Gooseberry R. indecorum Currant R. Roezlii Currant Plantanus racemosa Sycamore Rubus vitifolius Western Blackberry Cercocarpus ledifolius Mountain Mahogany C. betuloides Mountain Mahogany Adenostoma fasciculatum Greasewood Purshia glandulosa Antelope-brush Prunus virginiana Choke Cherry P. ilicifolia Holly-leaved Cherry Larrea divaricata Creosote Bush Rhus diversiloba Poisonoak R. trilobata Squaw Bush R. laurina Laurel Sumac R. integrifolia Lemonadeberry R. ovata Sugarbush Rhamnus crocea Buckthorn Ceanothus sp. Lilac C. cordulatus Snow-brush Fremontia californica California Slippery-elm Opuntia occidentalis Prickly-pear Arctostaphylos sp. Manzanita Salvia mellifera Black Sage S. apiana White Sage Lycium Andersonii Box-thorn Haplopappus squarosus Chrysothamnus nauseosus Rabbitbrush Baccharis sp. Mule Fat Franseria dumosa Burroweed Artemisia tridentata Basin Sagebrush A. californica Coastal Sagebrush Lepidospartum squamatum Scale-broom L. latisquamatum Scale-broom Tetradymia spinosa Cotton-thorn

Coastal Sage Scrub Association

MAJOR PLANTS

Artemisia californica Salvia apiana Salvia mellifera Eriogonum fasciculatum Rhus integrifolia Opuntia occidentalis Haploppapus squarrosus

This association is restricted to the Pacific base of the range, is typical on the alluvium at the bases of the coastal foothills, and usually grades into the chaparral at about 1800 feet elevation. When seen from above, the rather level terrain of the association is broken sharply at the mouths of canyons by dry washes, and is limited below, to the south, by cultivated land. The coastal sagebrush is the most characteristic plant of this association, occurring in all undisturbed parts of the area.

There are several habitats within the coastal sage scrub association. These differ from one another chiefly on the basis of soil type. The soil of the rather level sageland in most places is rocky or gravelly, or, as adjacent to washes, it is finely sandy in texture, and supports the major plants of the association. Most of the eroded adobe banks at the bases of the foothills support these same plants, with white sage being the dominant species. Locally, as in damp hollows or cleared areas, there is grassland. Jumbles of boulders, sand, gravel, and steep cutbanks, are characteristic of the channels of dry washes, these areas supporting sparse vegetation. The fauna and flora of the washes are distinct from those of surrounding sage flats. Because they are included within the geographic limits of the coastal sage belt, however, the washes are discussed along with this association.

The abruptness with which one habitat gives way to another in this association causes sharp dividing lines between the local ranges of certain mammals. For example, in trap lines transecting dry washes and level sageland two assemblages of rodents were found. That part of the line amid the boulders and cutbanks of the wash took mostly Peromyscus eremicus fraterculus and Neotoma lepida intermedia, while Perognathus fallax fallax, Dipodomys agilis agilis, and Peromyscus maniculatus gambeli were taken in the adjacent sage flats. The steep adobe slopes of the foothills, which constitute the upper part of the coastal sage scrub association, are commonly inhabited by Peromyscus californicus insignis, which rarely occurs in the level tracts of sage a few yards away. Thus, this association is not homogeneous with regard to its rodent population; many of these species have local and discontinuous distributions.

The following list gives the results of about 500 trap nights (a trap night equals one trap set out for one night) in typical coastal sage-scrub association one-half mile southwest of the mouth of San Antonio Canyon, at 1700 feet elevation.

TABLE 2.--YIELD OF 500 TRAP-NIGHTS IN THE COASTAL SAGE SCRUB ASSOCIATION.

	Number	Per cent of total
Perognathus fallax fallax	31	30.7
Dipodomys agilis agilis	20	19.8
Reithrodontomys megalotis longicaudus	4	4.0
Peromyscus californicus insignis	4	4.0
P. eremicus fraterculus	7	6.9
P. maniculatus gambeli	20	19.8
Neotoma lepida intermedia	9	8.8
N. fuscipes macrotis	2	2.0
Microtus californicus sanctidiegi	4	4.0

The list below indicates the catch in 200 trap nights in San Antonio Wash, at 1700 feet elevation and within the realm of the coastal sage; all of the traps were set in rocky and sandy main channels of the wash.

TABLE 3.--YIELD OF 200 TRAP-NIGHTS IN SAN ANTONIO WASH.

	Number	Per cent of total
Perognathus fallax fallax	2	5.1
Peromyscus californicus insignis	2	5.1
P. eremicus fraterculus	26	66.7
Neotoma lepida		

The prickly-pear cactus is of obvious importance to certain mammals of the coastal sage belt. This cactus is most common in disturbed areas such as sandy flats bordering washes, eroded adobe banks, and land once cleared by man. In these areas it is often the dominant plant with respect to area covered, usually growing in dense patches each covering approximately 150 square feet. It provides substitute nesting sites for Neotoma lepida in areas devoid of rock piles, and is probably the major factor governing the distribution of this wood rat in the sageland. Cottontails and brush rabbits use prickly-pear cactus extensively as refuge. Their forms and short burrows can be seen beneath many of the clumps of cactus.

This cactus serves as food for many mammals at least in the fruiting period in the fall. Usually only the fruit is eaten, but some pads are chewed by rabbits. The fruit or seeds of this plant are eaten by striped skunks, gray foxes, coyotes, pocket mice, kangaroo rats, wood rats, and probably white-footed mice.

The coyote is the dominant carnivore of the coastal sage flats. Many individuals spend the day in the adjacent chaparral-covered foothills and travel down into the flats at night to forage.

Southern Oak Woodland Association

MAJOR PLANTS

Alnus rhombifolia Quercus agrifolia Ribes indecorum Rhus integrifolia Rhus ovata Rhus trilobata

This association is limited to the Pacific slope of the mountain range, occurs in the mouths of canyons and on the floors of canyons, and extends up the larger canyons to 4000 feet elevation or higher. In a few areas on the flats at the coastal base of the range the oaks replace the coastal sage.

The large oaks forming an overhead canopy and the lack of much undergrowth give the oak woodland a shaded parklike appearance. Few brushy or herbaceous plants grow in the mull-laden soil beneath the oaks. Some grasses, however, are present locally.

Two habitats are found in the oak woodland: the pure oak woodland and the riparian. Much of the oak woodland is in canyons and therefore near streams or seepages. The larger streams have bordering growths of alders, willows, and blackberries, inhabited by meadow mice and shrews that are normally absent from the adjacent oak woodland. NEOTOMA FUSCIPES MACROTIS and PEROMYSCUS CALIFORNICUS INSIGNIS are commonly found in the riparian habitat, and Peromyscus boylii probably reaches peak abundance in the stream-side thickets and tangles of plant debris.

The rather open floor of the oak woodland is relatively devoid of mammal life. Peromyscus californicus and Peromyscus boylii, the only ground-dwelling rodents commonly found here, usually are taken near the limited areas of brushy growth, or the shelter afforded by logs and fallen branches. The paucity of shelter for small mammals seems to be an important factor limiting rodent populations in the oak woodland.

In the foothills of the San Gabriels the gray squirrel is restricted to the oak woodland, even though this association may be represented by only a narrow strip of canyon bottom oak trees. The presence or absence of "bridges" of oak woodland between mountains which are centers of gray squirrel populations and nearby ranges has probably been a major factor influencing the present geographic distribution of this animal.

The raccoon is the most abundant carnivore of the oak woodland, being especially common in the riparian habitat.

Chaparral Association

MAJOR PLANTS

Adenostoma fasciculatum Rhamnus crocea Quercus dumosa Cercocarpus betuloides Yucca Whipplei Prunus ilicifolia Ceanothus sp. Arctostaphylos sp. Umbellularia californica

This association is characteristic of the Pacific slope of the San Gabriels and extends from roughly 2000 feet elevation to 5000 or 6000 feet elevation. The ecotone between the chaparral and yellow pine forest associations covers a broad elevational belt, with chaparral following dry slopes up into coniferous forests, and conifers extending down north slopes surrounded by chaparral.

The chaparral association is characterized by tracts of dense brushy plants. These plants are from three to ten feet tall, their interlacing branches often forming nearly impenetrable thickets. Typically little herbaceous growth is present beneath the chaparral, the ground being covered with varying amounts of mull.

The effects of fire, slope, exposure, and elevation, make the chaparral association extremely varied with regard to habitats or plant formations. There are nearly pure stands of greasewood on the lower arid slopes; scrub oak, sumac, and lilac clothe less dry exposures; scrub oak and bay trees occur commonly amid granite talus; and locally groves of bigcone-spruce are found. Because of the many habitats present, and the difficulty of collecting in the chaparral, less was learned of the ecology of the mammals in this association than of those occurring elsewhere. The distribution of several chaparral-inhabiting mammals seems to be influenced by the distribution of locally characteristic plants, for example oak and bay woodland, or greasewood chaparral.

Several habitats within the chaparral community support few species of mammals and few individuals. Possibly the compact, rocky nature of the soil limits burrowing rodents, and the lack of herbaceous growth limits the food supply. Steep rocky slopes in San Antonio Canyon grown to mountain-mahogany and scrub oak were sparsely populated by Peromyscus boylii rowleyi, Peromyscus californicus insignis, and Neotoma fuscipes macrotis. Fifty traps set on such a slope for one night caught only three Peromyscus. Traps set in tracts of greasewood brush on dry south slopes at the head of Cow Canyon produced only California mice, Peromyscus californicus insignis Rhoads.

Following is a list of the mammals taken in the course of approximately 600 trap nights in the lower parts of the chaparral belt. All of the traps were set on slopes in San Antonio Canyon below 4000 feet elevation. The list gives a general indication of the relative numbers of rodents inhabiting one chaparral habitat: the arid greasewood-covered south slopes of the lower chaparral belt.

TABLE 4.--YIELD OF 600 TRAP-NIGHTS IN GREASEWOOD CHAPARRAL.

	Number	Per cent of total
Perognathus californicus dispar	4	10.0
Dipodomys agilis agilis	4	10.0
Peromyscus californicus insignis	25	62.5
Neotoma fuscipes macrotis	7	17.5

Heteromyids are evidently absent from the upper parts of the chaparral association, but cricetid rodents are common there beneath heavy clumps of lilac and in the talus beneath oaks and bay trees. The following list gives the mammals taken in the course of about 200 trap nights in the granite talus one half mile northwest of the mouth of Icehouse Canyon, at 5200 feet elevation.

TABLE 5.--YIELD OF 200 TRAP-NIGHTS IN THE UPPER PART OF THE CHAPARRAL ASSOCIATION.

	Number	Per cent of total

---------------+--------+---------- Eutamias merriami merriami | 3 | 6.3
Peromyscus boylii rowleyi | 38 | 79.2 Neotoma lepida intermedia | 2 | 4.2
Neotoma fuscipes macrotis | 5 | 10.4 ---
+--------+----------

The gray fox is the dominant carnivore of the chaparral association and forages widely in all habitats.

Yellow Pine Forest Association

MAJOR PLANTS

Pinus ponderosa P. lambertiana Libocedrus decurrens Abies concolor Quercus Kelloggii Ribes nevadense Ribes Roezlii Arctostaphylos sp. Ceanothus cordulatus

The crest of the range, from the upper limit of the chaparral association at roughly 6000 feet to the limited areas of boreal flora above 8500 feet elevation, is covered by yellow pine forests. On the desert slope of the range the coniferous forests which extend down to about 6000 feet represent the best development of this association, while the coniferous forests on the coastal side of the drainage divide are often more or less diluted by chaparral elements. For example, yellow pines on the Pacific face of Blue Ridge at 7000 feet elevation often grow in association with scrub oak and mountain-mahogany.

Few mammals are resident in the typical yellow pine forest as characterized by dense coniferous timber and little herbaceous or brushy growth. Here most of the species recorded actually find optimal conditions in an adjacent habitat. The forest probably harbors surplus individuals from adjacent preferred habitats, or, as in the case of chipmunks and ground squirrels, the forest often serves as forage ground while nearby brushy areas are utilized for breeding and shelter. The abundance of birds in the timber contrasts strikingly with the paucity of mammals there. The lack of a seed-producing understory, and the open duff-covered stretches of ground on which rodents would be extremely vulnerable to predation, probably in part account for the scarcity of rodents.

Within the general area encompassed by the yellow pine forest there are two major habitats, namely coniferous forest and chaparral. The species of plants comprising the chaparral of the Transition Life-zone are different from those comprising the chaparral of the Upper Sonoran Life-zone on the Pacific slope. In the chaparral of the Transition Life-zone, basin sagebrush and snowbrush grow in extensive patches in clearings in the timber. Dense thickets of choke cherry cover many damp hollows, and these thickets harbor the houses of Neotoma fuscipes. The food and shelter afforded by these chaparral areas importantly influence the local distribution of rodents: for example, Dipodomys agilis and Perognathus californicus in the yellow pine area are found only in association with chaparral, being completely absent from wooded areas.

The severe winter weather in this association must force many of the mammals into periods of inactivity. Probably during the long periods in the winter when snow covers the ground the heteromyids and sciurids remain below ground.

Pinyon-Juniper Woodland Association

MAJOR PLANTS

Pinus monophylla Juniperus californica Quercus dumosa var. turbinella Purshia glandulosa Fremontia californica Cercocarpus ledifolius Yucca Whipplei

In the San Gabriel Mountains this association is limited to the desert slope and reaches its lower limit at the bases of the foothills and extends up to the lower edge of the yellow pine forests. The altitudinal extent of the pinyon-juniper association is from roughly 4000 to 6000 feet elevation.

Several habitats are evident within the pinyon-juniper belt. On north slopes in the upper part of this association, scattered stands of pinyon pines are found with dense patches of scrub oak intervening, while on other such slopes a dense chaparral is present, consisting primarily of scrub oak, mountain-mahogany, and California slippery-elm. In this type of chaparral several hundred trap nights yielded only two rodent species: Neotoma fuscipes simplex and Peromyscus truei montipinoris. There are few pinyons on the south slopes, especially in the lower parts of the association; many of these slopes are clothed with an open growth of manzanita and yucca, while northern exposures there support mostly scrub oak. Many of the flats of the pinyon belt are grown to basin sagebrush.

Following is a list of the mammals taken in about 400 trap nights at one locality in the pinyon-juniper association. The area supported a mixed growth of pinyon, scrub oak, mountain-mahogany, and antelope-brush, together with smaller brushy plants, and was at the head of Grandview Canyon, at an altitude of roughly 5000 feet.

TABLE 6.--YIELD OF 400 TRAP-NIGHTS IN THE PINYON-JUNIPER ASSOCIATION.

	Number	Per cent of total
Perognathus fallax pallidus	3	11.5
Dipodomys agilis fuscus	9	34.6
Peromyscus truei montipinoris	10	38.5
Neotoma fuscipes simplex	4	15.4

Although Munz and Keck (1949:101) considered the pinyon-juniper belt as one association, on the desert slope of the San Gabriels pinyons and junipers do not generally grow on common ground; but rather the juniper belt represents a well defined habitat occurring between the pinyon covered slopes and the flats that support Joshua trees. Because the mammalian populations of the pinyon belt and the juniper belt are somewhat different, the mammals of these areas are most conveniently taken up separately.

In the juniper belt the juniper tree is of marked ecologic significance; the distribution of Peromyscus truei and Neotoma fuscipes is determined here by the presence of junipers. At certain times of year the fruit of this plant is eaten by coyotes, kangaroo rats, and wood rats.

The list below indicates the results of approximately 500 trap nights in the juniper belt near Mescal Canyon, between 4000 and 5000 feet elevation.

TABLE 7.--YIELD OF 500 TRAP-NIGHTS IN THE JUNIPER BELT.

	Number	Per cent of total
Perognathus fallax pallidus	16	16.7
Dipodomys merriami merriami	3	3.1
Dipodomys panamintinus mohavensis	36	37.5
Peromyscus truei montipinoris	22	22.9
Peromyscus maniculatus sonoriensis	12	12.5
Neotoma lepida lepida	2	2.1
Neotoma fuscipes simplex	2	2.1
Onychomys torridus pulcher	3	3.1

The biota of the washes that cut through the juniper belt in and below many of the larger canyons differs from that of the surrounding juniper-clad benches. Because the washes are in the same geographic area as the juniper belt they are discussed together. These washes on desert slopes are densely populated by rodents derived from adjacent areas, and support vegetation typical of higher floral belts in association with xerophytic, typically desert, species. In a sense, the washes serve to mix up the mammals of adjacent areas. For example, Onychomys torridus pulcher and Peromyscus eremicus eremicus, which are mammals typical of the desert, were found in Mescal Wash above their usual desert range; and Peromyscus californicus insignis and Peromyscus boylii rowleyi, which are chaparral inhabiting mammals, were found in the wash far removed from their chaparral environment. Washes are evidently effective agents in facilitating the dispersal of certain species of mammals. It is easy to envision a species crossing hostile habitats via dry washes to invade suitable niches in an area which is geographically and ecologically isolated from the original home of the species. Approximately 500 trap nights in Mescal Wash, at 4100 feet elevation, in the lower edge of the juniper belt, yielded the following mammals:

TABLE 8.--YIELD OF 500 TRAP-NIGHTS IN MESCAL WASH (DESERT SLOPE).

	Number	Per cent of total
Perognathus fallax pallidus	5	4.5
Dipodomys panamintinus mohavensis	43	38.7
Peromyscus californicus insignis	3	2.7
Peromyscus truei montipinoris	1	.9
Peromyscus boylii rowleyi	2	1.8
Peromyscus eremicus eremicus	28	25.0
Peromyscus maniculatus sonoriensis	23	20.5
Onychomys torridus pulcher	4	3.5
Neotoma lepida lepida	3	2.7

Dipodomys panamintinus mohavensis, Neotoma fuscipes simplex, and Peromyscus truei montipinoris are probably the most characteristic mammals of the pinyon-juniper association.

Sagebrush Scrub Association

MAJOR PLANTS

Bromus sp. Artemisia tridentata Chrysothamnus nauseosus Purshia glandulosa

This association is found on only the crest and desert slope of the range between 5000 and 8000 feet elevation. There it characteristically occupies flats and clearings in the yellow pine forest and pinyon-juniper woodland. The dominant plant of the association is basin sagebrush, and in many places this plant forms mixed growths with snowbrush and Haplopappus. The low brush of this association is formed by closely spaced bushes with grasses growing between.

Because of its limited occurrence in the San Gabriel Mountains, this association there has relatively little effect on mammalian distribution. Locally, nevertheless, the presence of this association governs the distribution of certain mammals. For example, on Blue Ridge, islands of sagebrush amid the conifers provide suitable habitat for Dipodomys agilis perplexus and Perognathus californicus bernardinus; and in Swarthout Valley D. a. perplexus, Reithrodontomys megalotis longicaudus, and Lepus californicus deserticola are seemingly restricted to the sagebrush flats.

Joshua Tree Woodland Association

MAJOR PLANTS

Yucca brevifolia Lycium Andersonii Eriogonum fasciculatum Tetradymia spinosa Ephedra sp. Larrea divaricata

This association is on the piedmont that dips toward the Mojave Desert from the interior base of the San Gabriels. The widely spaced Joshua trees with low bushes between, and the dry washes breaking the level terrain below the mouths of canyons are typical of this area. Field work was extended no farther down into the desert than about the 3500 foot level, where this association was still dominant.

Although the vegetation of this area is scattered and sparse, presenting a barren and sterile aspect, the area supports a rather high population of rodents. The soil at the bases of many large box-thorn- and creosote-bushes is perforated by burrow systems of Dipodomys panamintinus or Dipodomys merriami, and those burrows abandoned by kangaroo rats are used as retreats by Onychomys torridus and Peromyscus maniculatus. The mammals of this association are all characteristic of the fauna of the Mojave Desert, with the ranges of such species as the coyote and jack rabbit extending well up the desert slope of the mountains.

The mammals listed below were taken in 1948 in roughly 400 trap nights in the Joshua belt, at an elevation of 3500 feet, one mile below the mouth of Graham Canyon.

TABLE 9.--YIELD OF 400 TRAP-NIGHTS IN THE JOSHUA TREE BELT.

	Number	Per cent of total
Dipodomys panamintinus mohavensis	36	59.0
Dipodomys merriami merriami	15	24.6
Onychomys torridus pulcher	4	6.6
Peromyscus maniculatus gambeli	6	9.8

Populations of Dipodomys merriami and D. panamintinus fluctuate widely, possibly in response to weather cycles. In November of 1948 trapping in the Joshua belt showed that panamintinus outnumbered merriami approximately three to one, whereas in December of 1951, after a succession of unusually dry years, merriami was the more numerous. Further, merriami occurred in the lower parts of the juniper belt in 1951 where in 1948 it seemed to be absent.

Dipodomys merriami merriami and Onychomys torridus pulcher are diagnostic of the Joshua tree woodland association in the San Gabriel Mountains area, since few individuals of either species occur outside of this association.

ACCOUNTS OF SPECIES

Family DIDELPHIDAE

=Didelphis marsupialis virginiana= Kerr

Virginia Opossum

The opossum is common in and near small towns and cultivated areas at the Pacific base of the mountain range and does not thrive away from human habitation; extensive trapping in the coastal sage and chaparral belts produced no specimens except immediately adjacent to citrus groves. Pequegnat (1951:47) mentions that opossums in the Santa Ana Mountains of southern California are in the lower parts of the larger canyons, especially near human habitation.

Specimens examined.--Los Angeles County: Claremont, 1600 ft., 2 (PC).

Family TALPIDAE

=Scapanus latimanus occultus= Grinnell and Swarth

California Mole

Workings of moles were found on the Pacific slope of the mountains from 1600 feet at Claremont up to 7500 feet on Blue Ridge, and on the Pacific slope beneath basin sagebrush in Cajon Canyon one mile from desert slope Joshua-tree flats, but not on the desert slope, although moles probably occur on that slope in some of the places where there is suitable habitat.

Near Camp Baldy in the sandy soil beneath groves of alders moles seemed to be especially abundant. Although common on the coastal face of the range, moles shunned compact, dry, or rocky soils. In the greasewood chaparral one-half mile west of the mouth of Palmer Canyon, where the soil was hard and rocky, mole tunnels were in soft soil that had accumulated at the edge of a fire road beneath a steep road cut. The assumption is that this accumulation contained insects attractive, as food, to the moles.

Specimens examined, 2: Los Angeles County: Camp Baldy, 4200 ft., 1(PC); Claremont, 1600 ft., 1(PC).

Family SORICIDAE

=Sorex obscurus parvidens= Jackson

Dusky Shrew

Jackson (1928:124) recorded a specimen from Camp Baldy, 4200 feet, San Antonio Canyon.

=Sorex ornatus ornatus= Merriam

Ornate Shrew

Both of my specimens were taken amid riparian growth on the Pacific slope of the range.

Specimens examined, 2: Los Angeles County: San Antonio Canyon, 3500 ft., 1; Cobal Canyon, 5 mi. N Claremont, 1800 ft., 1 (PC).

=Notiosorex crawfordi crawfordi= (Coues)

Gray Shrew

One was taken in 1946 beneath a woodpile on the campus of Norton School, two miles northeast of Claremont, and examined by Dr. W. E. Pequegnat.

Family VESPERTILIONIDAE

=Myotis yumanensis sociabilis= H. W. Grinnell

Yuma Myotis

A female was taken in lower San Antonio Canyon, 2800 feet elevation, on

September 27, 1951.

=Myotis evotis evotis= (J. A. Allen)

Long-eared Myotis

This species was observed and collected at several stations ranging from 2800 feet elevation in San Antonio Canyon, to Blue Ridge at 8200 feet, and down the desert slope to 6000 feet at Jackson Lake. This distribution encompasses most of the chaparral and yellow pine forest associations. Within these areas, however, this bat shows marked habitat preferences.

Woodland habitats seem to be preferred by evotis. At several ponds in lower San Antonio Canyon this bat was observed repeatedly as it foraged over the water and coursed low between rows of alders and Baccharis. At Blue Ridge in September, 1951, these bats foraged approximately six feet above the ground beneath the canopy of coniferous foliage and between the trunks of the trees.

Most of the bats were taken by stretching fine wires above the surface of a pond as outlined by Borell (1937:478). Collecting was generally carried on until at least 11:00 p. m., and the time at which each bat was taken at the pond was recorded, thereby making possible a rough estimate of the pre-midnight forage period of each bat commonly collected at the ponds. Usually bats taken at the start of their supposed forage period had empty or nearly empty stomachs, whereas those taken towards the end of their forage period had full or nearly full stomachs. M. evotis usually first appeared just at dark, well after the pipistrelles and California myotis had begun foraging. The forage period of evotis seemed to begin approximately 30 minutes after sunset and to end approximately two and one-quarter hours later.

Individuals of this species were taken from May 4, to October 14, 1951. A female taken on May 19, 1951, in San Antonio Canyon, carried one minute embryo, and one taken in the same locality on June 8, had one embryo four millimeters in length.

Specimens examined.--Total, 12, distributed as follows: Los Angeles County: San Antonio Canyon, 2800 ft., 11; Claremont, 1100 ft., 1 (P.C.).

=Myotis volans interior= Miller

Interior Long-legged Bat

Although seldom found to be plentiful, this bat was recorded from many points on both the coastal and desert slopes of the mountains. Specimens were taken in the chaparral association in San Antonio Canyon, near Jackson Lake among yellow pines, and in Mescal Canyon at the upper limit of the Joshua tree woodland. Bats, probably volans, were noted over sage flats at 8000 feet elevation on Blue Ridge. The only place where these bats appeared to be numerous was Jackson Lake on the interior slope; there, on September 19, 1951, volans appeared with the pipistrelles, and was the most common bat before dark.

An individual of this species taken on October 28, 1951, in a short mine-shaft in the pinyon belt at the head of Grandview Canyon was slow in its movements and felt as cold as the walls of the tunnel. It was late afternoon and the temperature outside the cave was below 40 deg.F. The floor of the tunnel was covered with the hind wings of large moths of the genus Catocala; volans probably hung in the cave while eating them.

The series of volans from the San Gabriels shows that the two color phases of this bat both occur in the area. Two specimens from Jackson Lake contrast sharply with the rest of the series in their dark coloration. Benson (1949:50) states that color variation in a series of volans from a given locality may be striking.

This bat was collected in San Antonio Canyon from 50 minutes after sundown to two hours and 40 minutes after sundown. In this area these bats did not visit the ponds in large numbers as they seemed to do on the desert slope.

A female taken on May 29, 1951, contained one embryo nearly at term.

Specimens examined.--Total, 9, distributed as follows: Los Angeles County: Mescal Canyon, 8 mi. E and 5 mi. S Llano, 4900 ft., 1; 3 mi. W Big Pines, Swarthout Valley, 6000 ft., 3; San Antonio Canyon, 2800 ft., 5.

=Myotis californicus californicus= (Audubon and Bachman)

California Myotis

On the Pacific face of the mountain range this bat was recorded commonly below approximately 5000 feet elevation, where it seemed to be most common in the oak woodland of canyons. On the desert slope it was collected at Jackson Lake in yellow pine woodland, in Mescal Canyon in the juniper belt, and bats presumably of this species were observed at several points in the pinyon-juniper woodland.

Individuals of this species were often observed foraging from five to ten feet above the ground around the alders and Baccharis near San Antonio Creek, but they did not fly so low or so near the vegetation as did Myotis evotis. Here they were taken from 18 minutes to 55 minutes after sunset; this indicates an early and short forage period.

This bat may be active even in winter. On February 8, 1952, in lower San Antonio Canyon, a bat, probably of this species, was noted foraging; and collecting in early November, 1951, yielded specimens.

On May 22, 1951, a female obtained in San Antonio Canyon had one five-millimeter embryo, and subsequently all the females examined had embryos until June 12, when collecting was discontinued.

Specimens examined.--Total, 16, distributed as follows: Los Angeles County: Mescal Canyon, 4800 ft., 2; Jackson Lake, 6000 ft., 1 (PC); San Antonio Canyon, 3900 ft., 1; San Antonio Canyon, 2800 ft., 12.

=Pipistrellus hesperus merriami= (Dobson)

Western Pipistrelle

This is the most obvious if not the most common bat of the lower coastal slopes of the San Gabriels. In the spring and fall of 1951 individuals were noted from 1700 feet in the coastal sage scrub association to the white fir forests on Blue Ridge at 8200 feet elevation and were commonest in the rocky canyons of the lower Pacific slope below 4000 feet, and usually foraged near the steep canyon sides high above the canyon bottoms.

Pipistrelles were generally the first bats to appear in the evening, although the times of their appearance were irregular. In April and May, in lower San Antonio Canyon, they appeared from 28 minutes before sunset to 30 minutes after sunset, with the average time of appearance eight and one-half minutes after sunset. Like Myotis californicus this pipistrelle seemed to have a short and early foraging period. No pipistrelles were recorded at ponds later than one hour and five minutes after sunset, and usually they were not seen later than 40 minutes after sunset. Most of the specimens taken later than one half hour after sunset had full stomachs. More than 50 pipistrelles were captured at the ponds in San Antonio Canyon; six were kept for specimens. This species is probably present in the area throughout the winter. Pipistrelles were active in early April in Evey Canyon, were observed in early November in San Antonio Canyon, and on January 26, 1952, an individual was noted foraging near the mouth of Palmer Canyon. They are probably not active in winter on the colder desert slope of the mountains.

Pipistrelles often foraged in loose flocks of about half a dozen individuals. On many occasions these groups were first seen foraging high up above the canyon bottom, then, as it grew darker, they descended and foraged within 50 or 100 feet of the floor of the canyon. Immediately before dark these groups seemed to have forage beats; one minute several pipistrelles would be overhead, and the next minute none would be in sight.

A female taken in San Antonio Canyon on June 8, 1951, contained two five-millimeter embryos.

Specimens examined.--Total, 6, distributed as follows: Los Angeles County: San Antonio Canyon, 2800 ft., 5; Evey Canyon, 2400 ft., 1.

=Pipistrellus hesperus hesperus= (H. Allen)

Western Pipistrelle

This species was common in the spring and autumn of 1951 from the lower edge of the yellow pine forest down into the belt of Joshua trees. In early April on the desert slope at 4800 feet in Mescal Canyon, pipistrelles foraged on evenings when it was windy but not cold. On cold evenings (when the temperature was below roughly 45 deg.F) none was seen. On windy nights the pipistrelles often forsook their usual high forage habits and foraged 15 feet or so above the ground where the vegetation and outcrops of rock broke the force of the wind. In 1951 no pipistrelles were noted on the desert slope later than October 15.

Specimens examined.--Los Angeles County: Mescal Canyon, 4800 ft., 4.

=Eptesicus fuscus bernardinus= Rhoads

Big Brown Bat

This bat was on the coastal slope from the sage scrub association at 1100 feet, up to 8000 feet on Blue Ridge, and on the desert slope down to the upper edge of the Joshua tree belt at 4800 feet in Mescal Canyon. It was the most common bat at the ponds in San Antonio Canyon in May and June of 1951, but in

September and October of the same year none was obtained there.

On the Pacific slope of the San Gabriels the big brown bats segregate according to sex in the spring, the males occupying the foothills and mountains and the females the level valley floor at the coastal base of the range. Of 70 big brown bats captured in May and June of 1951, at the ponds in San Antonio Canyon, only one was a female. A large colony of more than 200 individuals in a barn near Covina, in the citrus belt, was composed of only females.

Times of capture of this bat at the ponds in San Antonio Canyon ranged from ten minutes after sunset to two hours and thirty minutes after sunset. Generally these bats came to the ponds in groups of several individuals, and often more than a dozen were captured in the course of an evening's collecting.

Specimens examined.--Total, 7, distributed as follows: Los Angeles County: Mescal Canyon, 4800 ft., 1; San Antonio Canyon, 2800 ft., 2; Covina, 1100 ft., 4 (2PC).

=Lasiurus borealis teleotis= (H. Allen)

Red Bat

One female was taken on September 30, 1951, in San Antonio Canyon, at 2800 feet elevation. The descriptions which the citrus growers of the Claremont and Glendora vicinity give of the bats they find occasionally hanging in their citrus trees accurately describe this species. Its seasonal occurrence there is unknown.

=Lasiurus cinereus cinereus= (Pasilot de Beauvois)

Hoary Bat

Specimens were collected in spring in 1951 at elevations of 2800 and 3200 feet in San Antonio Canyon, on the coastal slope, and in Mescal Canyon at 4900 feet, on the desert slope. Large, fast flying bats, probably of this species, were seen at Jackson Lake, 6000 feet elevation, on October 15, 1951.

Hoary bats are present in the San Gabriels in the fall, winter, and spring. In 1951 the last spring specimen was taken on June 11, in Mescal Canyon; then collecting was discontinued until late September when the first hoary bat was taken on the thirtieth of that month. From this date on into the winter hoary bats were recorded regularly. They seemed to be as common in early June as in most of April and May; possibly some remain in the San Gabriels throughout the summer.

In spring these bats seem to segregate by sex; of twelve kept as specimens and at least an equal number captured and released only one was a female. All were captured above 2800 feet.

Hoary bats seem to have a long pre-midnight forage period, having been captured at ponds from 21 minutes after sunset, to three hours and 26 minutes after sunset. Generally those taken early had empty stomachs and those taken later had full stomachs. On the night of May 24, 1951, a hoary bat captured two hours and five minutes after sunset had only a partially full stomach.

On May 25, 1951, an unusual concentration of hoary bats was observed at a pond at about 3200 feet elevation, in San Antonio Canyon (Vaughan, 1953). The day had been clear and warm, one of the first summerlike days of spring. Beginning at 30 minutes after sundown hoary bats were collected until two hours and 35 minutes after sundown; in this period 22 were caught and at least as many more observed. Many were released after being examined, whereupon they hung on the foliage of nearby alders to rest and dry themselves. This concentration of hoary bats may have been due to a sudden beginning of migration with a resultant concentration of bats at certain altitudinal belts. The warm weather might have set off the migration. On evenings that followed subsequent hot days no such concentration of hoary bats was seen. B. P. Bole (Hall 1946:156) observed a concentration of hoary bats on August 28, 1932, in

Esmeralda County, Nevada.

Several captive Myotis californicus in a jar next to a pond in San Antonio Canyon set up a squeaking which seemed to attract a hoary bat. Repeatedly the large bat swooped over the jar.

Specimens examined.--Total, 12, distributed as follows: Los Angeles County: Mescal Canyon, 4900 ft., 2; San Antonio Canyon, 3200 ft., 2; San Antonio Canyon, 2800 ft., 8.

=Antrozous pallidus pacificus= Merriam

Pallid Bat

The pallid bat is probably the most common and characteristic bat of the citrus belt at the Pacific base of the mountains. Only once, on May 4, 1951, was this bat taken in the mountains. On that night two individuals were collected at 2800 feet in San Antonio Canyon. All of the other specimens and observations were from colonies in old barns and outbuildings in the citrus belt where these bats are found in spring, summer, and fall.

The impression gained by examining many mixed colonies of Antrozous and Tadarida was that the former greatly outnumbered the latter. For example, a small colony of bats in an old barn near San Dimas Wash consisted of about thirty pallid bats and five freetails.

Large numbers of wings of moths of the family Sphingidae, and legs and parts of the heads of Jerusalem crickets (Stenopelmatus fuscus) were beneath an Antrozous night-roosting place in a barn near Upland.

Pallid bats were collected in 1951, from April 16 to October 17 but probably were active in the area into November.

Each of two pregnant females taken two miles northeast of San Dimas on

April 20, 1951, carried two embryos 4 millimeters long.

Specimens examined.--Total, 6, distributed as follows: Los Angeles County: 2 mi. NE San Dimas, 1200 ft., 2 (1PC); Ontario, 1100 ft., 4 (3PC).

Family MOLOSSIDAE

=Tadarida mexicana= (Saussure)

Mexican Free-tailed Bat

This bat, regularly met with in the citrus belt at the coastal base of the range, occurred in small numbers with colonies of Antrozous, and was once found with a colony of Eptesicus near Covina. None of the females taken in April 1951 was pregnant.

Specimens examined.--Los Angeles County: 2 mi. NE San Dimas, 1200 ft., 4.

=Eumops perotis californicus= (Merriam)

Mastiff Bat

H. W. Grinnell (1918:373) mentioned individuals collected at Sierra Madre (at the coastal base of the San Gabriels west of the study area), and Sanborn (1932:351) reported specimens from Covina and Azusa. Probably this bat occurs locally all along the coastal base of the range.

Family LEPORIDAE

=Lepus californicus bennettii= Gray

California Jack Rabbit

This species was found in the coastal sage belt from Cajon Wash west to San

Gabriel Canyon and was most plentiful in thin stands of sagebrush, and in and around citrus groves. Because of their preference for semi-open country, jack rabbits are absent from much of the coastal belt of sagebrush where the brush is fairly continuous, and they never were observed in the chaparral association.

Coyotes catch many jack rabbits and regularly forage around the foothill borders of the citrus groves for cottontails and jack rabbits.

A female examined on February 19, 1951, was pregnant, and one taken on March 15, 1951, carried three small embryos.

Specimens examined.--San Bernardino County: 2 mi. NW Upland, 1600 ft., 3 (PC).

=Lepus californicus deserticola= Mearns

California Jack Rabbit

There was sign of jack rabbits along the desert slope of the San Gabriels up to about 6700 feet, one-half mile west of Big Pines. They were fairly common in the Joshua tree belt, occurred less commonly in the juniper belt, and were present locally in small numbers in the pinyon-juniper association.

The population seemed to be at a low ebb from 1948 to 1952, when field work was done on the desert slope. I often hiked for an hour or more on the desert or juniper-covered benches without seeing a jack rabbit. The species was commoner in washes where as many as eleven were noted in two hours' hiking.

In December, 1951, below Graham Canyon, the leaves on large areas of many nearly recumbent Joshua trees had been gnawed down to their bases, and jack rabbit feces covered the ground next to these gnawings. Probably the Joshua tree is an emergency food used by the rabbits only when other food is scarce.

In years when the population of jack rabbits is not low they serve as a major food for coyotes. In the Joshua tree belt below Mescal Canyon, jack rabbit remains were fairly common in coyote feces, and tracks repeatedly showed where some coyote had pursued a jack rabbit for a short distance. A large male bobcat trapped in the juniper belt in Graham Canyon had deer hair and jack rabbit remains in its stomach.

Specimens examined.--Total, 7, distributed as follows: Los Angeles County: 6 mi. E and 1 mi. S Llano, 3500 ft., 4; Mescal Canyon, 4800 ft., 3.

=Sylvilagus audubonii sanctidiegi= (Miller)

Audubon Cottontail

Cottontails are common in the coastal sage scrub association and in and around citrus groves, but generally penetrate the mountains no farther than the lower limit of the chaparral association. They are everywhere on coastal alluvial slopes, except in the barren washes, and prefer patches of prickly-pear and often are loathe to leave its protection. After completely destroying a large patch of prickly-pear in the course of examining a wood rat house in the center of the cactus, I found hiding, in the main nest chamber of the house, a cottontail that dashed from its hiding place only when poked forceably with the handle of a hoe.

Cottontails are seldom above the sage belt in the chaparral associations, although along firebreaks and roads they occasionally occur there. Habitually cottontails escape predators in partly open terrain offering retreats such as low, thick brush, rock piles, and cactus patches; but on open ground beneath dense chaparral, cottontails may be vulnerable to predation.

Examinations of feces and stomach contents of the coyote reveals that it preys more heavily on cottontails than on any other wild species. Remains of several cottontails eaten by raptors were found in the sage belt.

In April, 1951, many young cottontails were found dead on roads in the sage belt, and a newly born cottontail was in the stomach of a coyote trapped four miles north of Claremont, on February 7, 1952.

Specimens examined.--Total, 3, distributed as follows: Los Angeles County: mouth of San Antonio Canyon, 2000 ft., 1 (PC). San Bernardino County: 2 mi. NW Upland, 1600 ft., 2 (PC).

=Sylvilagus audubonii arizonae= (J. A. Allen)

Audubon Cottontail

This subspecies was recorded on the interior slope from 5200 feet elevation, as at the head of Grandview Canyon, down into the desert, and was common in the sagebrush flats of the upper pinyon-juniper association. Piles of feces under thick oak and mountain-mahogany chaparral indicated that the rabbits often sought shelter there. Adequate cover is a requirement for this rabbit on the desert slope of the San Gabriels; in the juniper and Joshua tree belts the species occurs in washes where there is fairly heavy brush, and only occasionally elsewhere. In the foothills, when frightened from cover in one small wash cottontails often run up over an adjacent low ridge and seek cover in the brush of the next wash. In the wash below Graham Canyon tracks and observations showed that cottontails were taking refuge in deserted burrows of kit foxes.

In the pinyon-juniper association cottontails and jack rabbits probably occur in roughly equal numbers, but in the Joshua tree belt cottontails seem far less numerous than jack rabbits. In the course of a two hour hike in lower Mescal Wash, at about 3500 feet, eleven jack rabbits and two cottontails were noted.

Specimens examined.--Total, 2, distributed as follows: Los Angeles County: 6 mi. E and 1 mi. S Llano, 3500 ft., 1; Mescal Canyon, 4800 ft., 1.

=Sylvilagus bachmani cinerascens= (J. A. Allen)

Brush Rabbit

Brush rabbits inhabit the Pacific slope of the mountains from about 1200 feet in the coastal sagebrush belt up to at least 4500 feet in the chaparral, and are the only lagomorphs found commonly above the lower edge of the chaparral association. Here they were often on steep slopes beneath extensive and nearly impenetrable tracts of chaparral.

The ecologic niche of the brush rabbit is in brush where the plants form continuous thickets with little open ground. In the coastal sagebrush flats, areas supporting only scattered bushes are uninhabited by brush rabbits, while areas grown to extensive tracts of brush harbor them. When the brush rabbit's mode of escape from its enemies is considered, the reason for their habitat preference becomes more clear. Almost invariably these rabbits seek escape by running through the densest portions of the brush, never appearing in the open; in this way they travel quickly away from the source of danger without being observed. Because they avoid being seen in the open, and do not seek safety largely through running ability, they need continuous stretches of brush for escape. While hunting in the coastal sagebrush belt I have repeatedly seen frightened brush rabbits turn and dart beneath the bushes a few feet from a human being rather than be driven into the open.

A great horned owl shot in March, 1951, in the sage belt, had in its stomach the remains of a freshly killed adult brush rabbit. Although coyotes and brush rabbits often occur in the same general sections of the sage flats, remains of these rabbits have been notably scarce in coyote feces from these areas. This is probably because the coyote hunts along clearings and in open brushland, precisely the type of habitat avoided by brush rabbits.

Family SCIURIDAE

=Sciurus griseus anthonyi= Mearns

Western Gray Squirrel

Gray squirrels were on both slopes of the San Gabriels in oak woodland. A gray squirrel was observed in April of 1948, as it climbed a telephone pole adjacent to an orange grove near Cucamonga. This, and one noted bounding up a slope of greasewood chaparral near Cattle Canyon, were the only gray squirrels seen in areas which were not grown to oaks or adjacent to oak woodland. In the lower foothills gray squirrels were invariably found in association with valley oak, this plant forming limited woodland areas in canyon bottoms. In the upper chaparral association the squirrels frequented the large scrub oaks growing on talus slopes and canyon sides. In the yellow pine woodland, gray squirrels are restricted to black oaks, often where they formed mixed stands with the conifers. On the interior slope these squirrels were found only at the lower edge of the yellow pine woodland where black oaks are common. There, in the vicinity of Big Pines, they were present between roughly 5800 and 7000 feet, while on the Pacific slope they inhabited oak woodland from 1600 feet to about 7000 feet elevation.

In Live Oak Canyon in December of 1950, tracks indicated that a bobcat had killed a gray squirrel in a small draw beneath the oaks. In Evey Canyon on March 6, 1951, while watching for bats at late twilight, I observed a gray squirrel traveling through the branches of a nearby oak. A great horned owl glided into the oak in an attempt to catch the squirrel, which leaped quickly into a dense mass of foliage and escaped. For roughly ten minutes the owl perched in the oak watching its intended prey, then flew off down the canyon amid frantic scolding by the squirrel.

On March 17, 1951, a female gray squirrel taken at about 3500 feet elevation in San Antonio Canyon contained two embryos, each roughly 40 millimeters long.

=Spermophilus beecheyi beecheyi= (Richardson)

Beechey Ground Squirrel

From the coastal sage belt, into the yellow pine forest of the Pacific slope, this species is common on land cleared by man or disturbed in the course of construction, or on severely eroded slopes where the original climax vegetation is partly or completely absent. Thus in the sage belt, ground squirrels live along dirt roads through the brush, on the heavily eroded banks often found in the foothills, on land grazed closely by sheep, and in those parts of major washes such as San Antonio and Cucamonga washes where scatterings of huge boulders offer prominent vantage points. In San Antonio Canyon Spermophilus was restricted to the vicinity of roads and firebreaks, and an especially large colony of at least forty individuals lived at a dump one mile southwest of Camp Baldy at about 4500 feet elevation. Ground squirrels used burned stems of large laurel sumac as observation posts. Because of a preference for open areas offering unobstructed outlooks, ground squirrels originally probably did not penetrate the main belt of heavy chaparral on the Pacific slope of the range except in some of the large washes.

In the spring of 1951 and the preceding summer there was a marked increase in the ground squirrel population near Padua Hills as a result of sheep grazing on approximately one-half square mile of sage land. Grasses and smaller shrubs were eaten down to the ground, and in some places coastal sagebrush and Haplopappus were killed by browsing and trampling. The area formerly had a sparse growth of bushes with intervening growths of tall grasses and one colony of perhaps 20 ground squirrels; but after the sheep grazing the area was open brushland with large clear spaces on which the herbage was trimmed to the ground, and had at least four colonies of ground squirrels as large as the first. Also there were other ground squirrels established in various parts of the area. Probably the dry weather in the winter of 1950-51 with consequent retardation of the vegetation aided the spread of the squirrels in this area.

In the sage belt, most ground squirrels are dormant by December. In 1951, after a mild winter, squirrels were noted on January 25 near Padua Hills. On February 8, 1951, males in breeding condition were collected, and on March

16, a female taken near San Antonio Wash carried three small embryos. In early March of 1951, ground squirrels were active at 4500 feet elevation in San Antonio Canyon.

Specimen examined.--Los Angeles County: 1 mi. S and 2 mi. E Big Pines, 8000 ft., 1.

=Spermophilus beecheyi fisheri= (Merriam)

California Ground Squirrel

This ground squirrel inhabited the desert slope of the mountains up to 5000 feet elevation, and was most common in the juniper belt; burrows often were made under large junipers. In May, 1949, ground squirrels were common in the rocks adjacent to Mescal Wash at an elevation of 4500 feet. In an apple orchard near Valyermo, squirrels fed on the fallen fruit in early November of 1951.

No squirrel was seen in December, January, and February, indicating that all were below ground in winter.

Specimen examined.--San Bernardino County: Desert Springs, 4000 ft., 1 (PC).

=Ammospermophilus leucurus leucurus= (Merriam)

Antelope Ground Squirrel

Antelope ground squirrels were common in the Joshua tree woodland where they were noted up to 4500 feet elevation in Graham Canyon. None was found on the pinyon slopes, possibly because of the competition offered there by Eutamias merriami, or because the rocky nature of the soil there rendered burrowing difficult.

Although observed less often in winter than in summer, this species is active all year. On February 6, 1949, in Mescal Wash, an antelope ground squirrel was foraging over the snow which was at least six inches deep. These squirrels were attracted to the carcasses of rodents used as bait for carnivore sets, and caused a good deal of trouble by disturbing the traps.

Antelope ground squirrels used the topmost twigs of box-thorn bushes extensively as lookout posts, and many of their burrows were at the bases of these thorny bushes. This habit of regularly using observation posts is well developed in each species of ground squirrel found in the San Gabriels.

Specimens examined.--Los Angeles County: 6 mi. E and 1 mi. S Llano, 3500 ft., 2.

=Eutamias speciosus speciosus= (Merriam)

Lodgepole Chipmunk

This chipmunk was characteristic of the most boreal parts of the San Gabriel Mountains. It was recorded from 6800 feet elevation at Big Pines, to an altitude of approximately 9800 feet near Mt. San Antonio, and was common where coniferous timber was interspersed with snowbrush chaparral. In upper Icehouse Canyon and near Telegraph Peak these chipmunks were associated with lodgepole pines and chinquapin, and one mile east of Mt. San Antonio individuals were often observed in thickets of manzanita. This chipmunk usually shunned pure stands of coniferous timber except as temporary forage ground.

On Blue Ridge these chipmunks used the uppermost stems of snowbrush as vantage points, and when disturbed ran nimbly over thorny surfaces of the brush in seeking refuge in the tangled growth.

In early November of 1951, these animals were not yet in hibernation on Blue Ridge. They were noted on November 6, after the season's first snows had melted; on November 13, however, a cold wind with drifting fog kept most of them under cover, and only two were noted in the course of the day.

Specimen examined.--Los Angeles County: 1 mi. S and 2 mi. E Big Pines, 8100 ft., 1.

=Eutamias merriami merriami= (J. A. Allen)

Merriam Chipmunk

The lower limit of the range of this species, on the coastal face of the range, is roughly coincident with that of manzanita--that is to say, it begins in the main belt of chaparral above the lower foothills. E. merriami seems to reach maximum abundance amid the granite talus, and scrub oak and Pseudotsuga growth at the upper edge of the chaparral association. It was absent, however, from all but the lower fringe of the yellow pine forest association.

On the desert slope merriami was partial to rocky areas in the pinyon-juniper association but was also in the black oak woods on the Ball Flat fire road near Jackson Lake. Nowhere was Eutamias merriami and E. speciosus observed on common ground.

Specimens examined.--Los Angeles County: San Antonio Canyon, 5500 ft., 2 (1 PC).

=Glaucomys sabrinus californicus= (Rhoads)

Northern Flying Squirrel

No specimens of this species were taken in the field work in the San Gabriels, nor did I find any rangers or residents of the mountains who had seen flying squirrels in the area. Nevertheless sign found in the white fir forests in the Big Pines area indicated that flying squirrels may occur there. On a number of occasions dissected pine cones were noted on the horizontal limbs and bent trunks of white firs. These cones were too large to have been carried there by chipmunks, and gray squirrels were often completely absent from the areas. I suspect that extensive trapping in the coniferous forests of the higher parts of the mountains would produce specimens of flying squirrels. Willett (1944:19) mentions that flying squirrels probably occur in the San Gabriel Mountains.

Family GEOMYIDAE

=Thomomys bottae pallescens= Rhoads

Valley Pocket Gopher

This gopher was found below about 5000 feet elevation in disturbed or open areas from Cajon Wash at Devore westward all along the coastal base of the San Gabriel Range. In the lower part of the chaparral belt the gopher evidently was absent from the chaparral-covered slopes, but was common along roads and on fire trails.

Burt (1932) and von Bloeker (1932) discuss the distribution of the three subspecies of this species, pallescens, neglecta, and mohavensis, which are in the San Gabriel Mountains area, and Burt indicates that pallescens grades toward mohavensis in the southern part of Antelope Valley.

=Thomomys bottae neglectus= Bailey

Valley Pocket Gopher

In the forests of yellow pine and white fir of the higher parts of the San Gabriel Mountains the workings of this gopher were common, and sign of its presence was found above 4500 feet on both slopes of the mountain range. The rocky character of the coastal slope seems to limit the occurrence of gophers, for they are not continuously distributed there. On the desert slope they occur locally down into the pinyon-juniper belt.

In the vicinity of Big Pines, on the interior slope, these gophers preferred broken forest where snow brush or other brush occurred; their workings, however, were also found beneath groves of conifers and black oaks. The abundance of earth cores resting on the duff indicated that this species is active in the snow in winter.

Specimens examined.--Total, 5, distributed as follows: Los Angeles County: 2 mi. E Valyermo, 4600 ft., 2; 3 mi. W Big Pines, 6000 ft., 1; 1 mi. S and 2 mi. E Big Pines, 8000 ft., 2.

=Thomomys bottae mohavensis= Grinnell

Valley Pocket Gopher

One specimen of this subspecies was taken on December 31, 1951, in the Joshua tree belt, eight miles east of Llano, 3700 feet elevation.

Family HETEROMYIDAE

=Perognathus fallax fallax= Merriam

San Diego Pocket Mouse

This pocket mouse is restricted to the coastal sage scrub association, and was recorded from Cajon Wash west to Live Oak Canyon. The mouse does not inhabit even the lower edge of the chaparral belt, but in the coastal sage flats is usually the most abundant rodent. In disturbed parts of the coastal sage belt fallax is less common, and was never trapped in channels of rocky washes. Trap lines in the eroded adobe banks of the foothills, where white sage and coastal sagebrush are the dominant plants, took mostly these pocket mice. Although the soil of such slopes is compact and seemingly is unsuitable for burrowing by heteromyids, fallax is the most common rodent. Because few burrows of pocket mice were noted there, it is possible that the many old unused burrows of Spermophilus and Dipodomys which honeycomb certain parts of adobe banks are used also by fallax; some of these burrows shelter Peromyscus eremicus and Peromyscus californicus.

These mice are inactive above ground in cold weather. In the sage belt near Thompson Canyon, where this subspecies had been found to be the most common rodent, none was trapped on the sub-freezing night of December 3, 1948, although other rodents were found in usual numbers. Individuals have been taken on nights of intermittent rain, yet none has been trapped on freezing nights.

This species is characteristically heavily infested by a large species of mite. Usually these mites congregate around the base of the tail.

On October 11, 1949, one lactating female and two carrying embryos were taken.

Specimens examined.--Total, 11, distributed as follows: Los Angeles County: 4 mi. N and 1 mi. E Claremont, 1900 ft., 5; 3 mi. N Claremont, 1600 ft., 6 (5 PC).

=Perognathus fallax pallidus= Mearns

San Diego Pocket Mouse

On the desert slope of the mountains this species is found in the part of the pinyon-juniper association that is between elevations of 4000 and 5200 feet. The mouse is absent from the higher chaparral and pinyon-covered slopes, but is present on south slopes in the pinyon belt where more open growths of pinyons and scrub oaks are interspersed with yucca. I recorded this pocket mouse from the vicinity of Cajon Pass west to Valyermo.

The local distribution of pallidus is striking because of its close positive correlation with the distribution of yucca. On benches around 5000 feet, where yuccas are scattered in their occurrence, pallidus is nearly always taken near (often right at the base of) this plant. Lower in the juniper belt the dry rocky south slopes supporting yucca plants are well populated by pallidus, while adjacent flats, and north slopes grown to antelope brush and scrub oak, are completely uninhabited. Near the mouth of Grandview Canyon, on steep rocky southern exposures grown sparsely to burro weed and yucca, one hundred traps produced in one night eight pallidus and no other rodents. Here many of these pocket mice were trapped on large fractured rock outcroppings, where most or all of the mice probably lived in the daytime in the deep cracks; in any event no burrows were noted near these rocks.

This species prefers barren slopes supporting yucca plants. These plants produce large seeds which are staple food items for P. f. pallidus and other rodents during the lean part of the year, that is to say, late summer and autumn. Many of the dry capsules of the yucca plants were examined in October, 1951, and these generally still contained a few seeds. Pocket mice taken in October usually carried in their cheek pouches seeds of yucca together with some other material, and often they carried only the seeds of yucca. Probably the wind shakes only a few seeds out of the capsules at a time, thus tending to drop the seeds over a fairly long period.

Trapping in winter in the juniper belt revealed that these pocket mice were not active above ground on nights colder than about 40 deg. F. On nights when the temperature was about 36 deg. F. none was taken, but on the one night in late December, 1948, when the minimum was 44 deg. F., several specimens were taken. In this same area in May 1949, pocket mice were the most numerous rodents. Because of their evident sensitivity to cold weather, these mice must remain below ground for weeks at a time during the cold weather of December and January.

Specimens of pallidus from the desert slope of the San Gabriels are grayer (less brown) than specimens taken farther southeast in the Mojave and Colorado deserts. Further sampling of populations of Perognathus fallax from areas adjacent to the San Gabriels might demonstrate differences of sufficient magnitude to warrant subspecific distinction of the San Gabriel population.

Possibly, however, the San Gabriel series manifests only local variation in the race pallidus. Grinnell (1933:54) characterizes the ecological niche of the race pallidus as being "open, sandy ground, often ... surrounded by rocky slopes," whereas these pocket mice in the San Gabriels inhabited gravelly or rocky juniper-dotted benches.

Specimens examined.--Total, 11, distributed as follows: Los Angeles County: 5 mi. E and 4 mi. S Llano, 4500 ft., 7; 2 mi. E Valyermo, 4500 ft., 3; 4 mi. E Valyermo, 5000 ft., 1.

=Perognathus californicus dispar= Osgood

California Pocket Mouse

Mice of this subspecies were recorded from the lower chaparral association below about 4000 feet elevation along the coastal face of the San Gabriel Range. They were trapped on greasewood-covered slopes, in mixed growths of white sage and buckwheat, and beneath scrub oak and lilac chaparral; however none was taken in the heavy chaparral of the upper parts of the chaparral association.

One small juvenile in gray pelage was taken in San Antonio Canyon on October 1, 1951.

Specimens examined.--Total, 5, distributed as follows: San Bernardino County: Lytle Canyon, 4000 ft., 2 (PC). Los Angeles County: San Antonio Canyon, 3000 ft., 3.

=Perognathus californicus bernardinus= Benson

California Pocket Mouse

On Blue Ridge these mice were recorded between 7100 and 8000 feet elevation. Here they were restricted to dense tracts of snowbrush and sagebrush, often where these tracts were interspersed with, or beneath, open groves of conifers. These mice seemed to favor areas where this thick brush was broken by patches of open, grass-covered ground. Benson (1930:450) records this subspecies from Swarthout Valley, near Big Pines, at 6860 feet elevation.

While setting traps for pocket gophers one mile southwest of Big Pines, in September of 1951, I frightened a pocket mouse from its burrow. The animal jumped into the tangle of interlacing twigs of a nearby clump of snowbrush, and with great dexterity climbed into the center of the bush, where it was lost to view. I was surprised at the facility with which this saltatorial rodent traveled through the network of small branches.

In winter, in areas inhabited by this mouse, snow covers the ground for long periods during which these mice are probably forced to remain below ground.

Specimens examined.--Los Angeles County: 1 mi. S and 2 mi. W Big Pines, 7400 ft., 2.

=Dipodomys panamintinus mohavensis= (Grinnell)

Panamint Kangaroo Rat

This rat is common in the Joshua tree and juniper belts, and locally penetrates the pinyon belt at about 5000 feet elevation. It occurs regularly along the entire desert slope of the San Gabriel Mountains.

The upper limit of the range of this species roughly coincides with the upper limit of the juniper belt, and within this range it was found to inhabit areas having widely different soil types. It occurred on the sandy ground of desert washes, the gravelly soil of the juniper-clad benches, and the mixed sandy and rocky ground of washes in canyons. A preference is shown by panamintinus for fairly level ground. Rough terrain or steep slopes are generally avoided, whereas rather large colonies of these kangaroo rats are found in small flats of the desert foothills.

Below about 4500 elevation on the interior slope this species was the most numerous rodent, and seemed to reach maximum abundance in the Joshua tree association. About 500 trap-nights in the juniper belt near Graham Canyon yielded 31 specimens, whereas about 300 trap-nights in Joshua tree flats took 34 individuals.

The cheek pouches of many specimens taken in early winter contained green shoots of grass and little dry material. On many occasions rat traps set next to wood rat nests beneath large junipers produced panamintinus, and many of these animals had their cheek pouches crammed full of juniper berries.

In December, 1948, panamintinus was trapped consistently on nights when the temperature dropped to below 20 deg. F. On December 27, 1948, after a three inch snowfall, tracks of this species were noted in the snow at the mouth of Mescal Canyon.

Parts of the skulls of this species were found in many coyote feces from the desert slope.

Specimens examined.--Total, 11, distributed as follows: Los Angeles County: Mescal Wash, 4000 ft., 8 (6 PC); 2 mi. E Valyermo, 4600 ft., 3.

=Dipodomys merriami merriami= Mearns

Merriam Kangaroo Rat

This kangaroo rat barely enters the area under consideration and is almost restricted to the Joshua tree association, for only a few individuals were taken at the lower edge of the juniper benches. This species inhabits the Joshua tree belt all along the desert base of the San Gabriels.

As mentioned in the description of the Joshua tree association, the relative numbers of Dipodomys merriami and D. panamintinus shifted from 1948 to 1951, possibly concurrent with the seasons of low rainfall in this period. Whereas in 1948 merriami was decidedly less abundant than panamintinus in the Joshua tree belt, in 1951 the numbers were reversed.

In December, 1951, it was found by tending the traps in the early evening that merriami foraged fairly early before the ground had frozen solidly.

Specimens examined.--Los Angeles County: 2 mi. NW mouth of Graham Canyon, 3500 ft., 5 (PC).

=Dipodomys merriami parvus= Rhoads

San Bernardino Kangaroo Rat

One specimen of this subspecies was trapped on November 26, 1951, in a sandy channel of Cajon Wash near Devore beneath a clump of scale-broom.

=Dipodomys agilis agilis= Gambel

Pacific Kangaroo Rat

This species was found below about 4000 feet elevation all along the coastal face of the range and reached maximum abundance in the level tracts of coastal sage. It was one of the most abundant rodents there, usually being second to Perognathus fallax in point of numbers. Large colonies of kangaroo rats occurred locally on sandy ground adjacent to large washes. The rats were found sparingly on the foothill adobe banks and in the greasewood chaparral of the lower foothills, but in heavy chaparral where a layer of plant debris covered the ground, such as on north slopes grown to scrub oak and lilac, kangaroo rats were completely absent. Thus, in the lower chaparral belt, this rodent had a discontinuous distribution.

The coyote probably is one of the major predators of these kangaroo rats;

remains of this rodent were often found in coyote feces, and coyotes excavated many burrow systems in large kangaroo rat colonies in the sandy ground near San Antonio Wash. The soil there is so soft that coyotes probably were often successful in digging out their prey. The shed skin of a large Pacific rattlesnake (Crotalus viridis helleri) was found four feet inside the mouth of a kangaroo rat burrow; probably this reptile preys on agilis. Great horned owls (Bubo virginianus pacificus) come down nightly from the chaparral to hunt in the sage flats. Beneath the perches of these owls I have found pellets containing bones of agilis.

Specimens examined.--Total, 13, distributed as follows: Los Angeles County: San Antonio Wash, 1900 ft., 11 (10 PC); 4 mi. NE Claremont, 1600 ft., 2.

=Dipodomys agilis perplexus= (Merriam)

Pacific Kangaroo Rat

All the specimens of this species from the desert slope of the San Gabriel Range are referred to the subspecies perplexus. They were taken in brushy habitats between the elevations of 4500 and 7400 feet. Throughout much of this area perplexus was found only in certain restricted areas more or less surrounded by inhospitable ground. For example, at 7400 feet on Blue Ridge, they were found occasionally in the strips of sagebrush and lilac brush which locally capped this ridge. Often these patches of chaparral on Blue Ridge were surrounded by areas unsuitable for kangaroo rats: on the Pacific slope, talus, oaks, and yellow pines prevailed; on the ridge scattered yellow pine groves were present; and on the steep desert slope there were yellow pines and white firs. In Swarthout Valley perplexus was found in flats that supported basin sagebrush and Haploppus, while the coniferous forests to the south, and pinyon-covered slopes to the north were uninhabited. On flats supporting antelope brush and juniper, perplexus was often common, but it did not penetrate the chaparral of adjacent slopes grown to scrub oak and mountain-mahogany. In general then, perplexus was found in fairly open brushy flats or slopes, even where these were surrounded by unsuitable habitats.

Specimens of D. agilis from the desert slope two miles east of Valyermo are referrable to the subspecies perplexus. A series taken in Cajon Wash at Devore, on the Pacific slope, is intermediate between agilis, of the coastal slope of the San Gabriels, and perplexus of the desert slope, but approaches more nearly the later subspecies. Thus, different subspecies of D. agilis occur on opposite slopes of the San Gabriel Mountains, with intergradation taking place in the Cajon Pass area and probably also at the west end of the Mountains.

Both scrub oak acorns and juniper berries were found in the cheek pouches of this subspecies, and one immature individual taken in Swarthout Valley had its cheek pouches stuffed with approximately 550 seeds of brome grass.

On November 13, 1951, at 7500 feet on Blue Ridge, a small juvenile was taken; it must have been born not earlier than September.

Specimens examined.--Total, 17, distributed as follows: Los Angeles County: 2 mi. E Valyermo, 4600 ft., 3; 5 mi. E Valyermo, 1; 1 mi. E Big Pines, 6600 ft., 6; 1 mi. S and 2 mi. W Big Pines, 7400 ft., 2. San Bernardino County: Cajon Wash, 1/2 mi. SW Devore, 2200 ft., 5.

Family CRICETIDAE

=Reithrodontomys megalotis longicaudus= (Baird)

Western Harvest Mouse

This species inhabited grassy areas of the coastal sage belt, and reached maximum abundance on cleared land grown thickly to weeds and scattered brush. The mouse was only locally abundant--being scarce throughout much of the sage belt--but was found under contrasting conditions. In San Antonio Wash the species was taken among rocks and sparse weeds, at Palmer Canyon specimens were trapped on a barren ridge sparsely clothed with greasewood and white sage, and also one mile E of Big Pines in flats supporting basin sagebrush and a fairly dense growth of grasses. The western harvest mouse was recorded from 1500 feet elevation to 3200 feet on the Pacific slope, and at 6600 feet near Big Pines on the desert slope.

Those specimens of harvest mice from near Big Pines may be grading toward the desert race megalotis; my series of specimens from this locality, however, is too small for clear indications on this point.

Individuals in juvenal pelage were taken on November 26, 1951, near Devore.

Specimens examined.--Total, 6, distributed as follows: Los Angeles County: 1 mi. E Big Pines, 6600 ft., 2; Palmer Canyon, 2000 ft., 1; 4 mi. N Claremont, 1700 ft., 3 (PC).

=Peromyscus eremicus eremicus= (Baird)

Cactus Mouse

In Mescal Wash on the desert slope of the San Gabriels, this mouse was one of the most abundant mammals and was the only rodent other than Peromyscus maniculatus regularly trapped in the barren channels of washes. In Mescal Wash, at an altitude of 4000 feet, eremicus occurred along with the chaparral-inhabiting Peromyscus boylii and Peromyscus californicus. The two species last mentioned were associated with the occasional large patches of manzanita, antelope brush, and other brush of the wash, whereas eremicus was trapped in the rocky and sandy channels among scattered bushes of scale-broom. No specimens of eremicus were taken on the juniper-clad benches adjacent to the wash.

Specimens examined.--Los Angeles County: Mescal Wash, 4000 ft., 10 (4 PC).

=Peromyscus eremicus fraterculus= (Miller)

Cactus Mouse

This mouse was recorded from 1900 feet elevation, one mile south of the mouth of San Antonio Canyon, to 3200 feet elevation in Cajon Canyon. This subspecies is characteristic of the sage belt and shows a strong preference for the rough rocky areas found in dry washes. Although in many areas the channels of the washes are immediately adjacent to sandy sagebrush-covered flats, eremicus is not common in the latter areas. Rocks seem to be essential to eremicus, for sandy areas in the sageland which were devoid of rocks yielded only an occasional specimen. For example, 100 trap-nights in the main channel of San Antonio Wash yielded 23 eremicus and only six other rodents; while in the sandy sage areas nearby 200 trap-nights yielded only one eremicus and 32 other rodents.

In lower San Antonio Canyon eremicus seemed restricted to the rocky canyon bottom, none having been trapped on the steep slopes nearby. This subspecies occurs commonly, however, on the adobe banks grown to white sage at the base of the foothills. There eremicus occurred on common ground with Perognathus fallax fallax, and was often the only Peromyscus taken.

This species may be restricted by temperature; washes above 4000 feet elevation, which seemed suitable were uninhabited by these mice.

On December 1, 1949, two females taken at the mouth of Palmer Canyon had well advanced embryos. A female trapped in San Antonio Canyon on September 19, 1951, was lactating. Juveniles were caught in the sage belt in October, 1951.

Specimens examined.--Total, 6, distributed as follows: Los Angeles County: San Antonio Canyon, 2500 ft., 1; San Antonio Wash, 1800 ft., 5 (PC).

=Peromyscus californicus insignis= Rhoads

California Mouse

This mouse inhabits areas supporting chaparral on the coastal slope of the San Gabriels below 5000 feet. In the chaparral it is usually the most plentiful rodent, being dominant on slopes which have been burned over and on which greasewood chaparral has taken over. On one such slope at the head of Cow Canyon, at 4500 feet, this was the only rodent trapped, although an occasional wood rat house was noted. Trapping records gave the impression that this form was the most ubiquitous rodent in the entire chaparral belt. Nearly every trap line, even in such non-productive areas as oak woodland, took the California mouse; and in many areas, as in thick lilac brush, this mouse was by far the most abundant rodent. Specimens were taken on the damp ground next to San Antonio Creek, and in the riparian growth. In San Antonio Wash the California mouse was found in thickets of laurel sumac and lemonade berry, or other large shrubs, but were absent from most of the adjacent sageland. The one place where they were found away from heavy brush was on a series of barren adobe banks, near Palmer Canyon, clothed mostly with white sage. Here they found shelter in the unused burrows of kangaroo rats and ground squirrels.

The only place on the desert slope where this species was taken was in Mescal Wash. There it was taken occasionally near the large clumps of antelope-brush and manzanita which grew in the main channels of the wash.

Lactating females of this species were taken in October, 1949, and February, 1950. Two pregnant females were trapped on February 25, 1950, at the mouth of Palmer Canyon.

Specimens examined.--Total 16, distributed as follows: Los Angeles County: Mescal Wash (4200 ft., 4; 4300 ft., 1; 4500 ft., 1), 6(2IM); San Antonio Canyon, 4500 ft., 1; San Antonio Canyon, 3000 ft., 5; mouth of Palmer Canyon, 1900 ft., 4 (PC).

=Peromyscus maniculatus gambeli= (Baird)

Deer Mouse

This species occurs from 1000 feet elevation to above 9000 feet elevation on the Pacific slope of the Mountains, but although probably the most widespread rodent in the area it is absent from many habitats. This mouse reaches maximum abundance in the coastal sage scrub association, particularly where the soil is sandy with scattered vegetation--usually coastal sagebrush and black sage. On the foothill adobe slopes none was trapped, nor have any been taken in most of the chaparral habitats. A few gambeli were trapped amid the talus beneath growths of scrub oak and bay trees in San Antonio Canyon, at 4300 feet elevation. On Blue Ridge, at elevations of from 7200 feet to 8300 feet, this mouse inhabited areas clothed with snowbush, basin sagebrush, currant, and scattered conifers, and was found sparingly in the coniferous forests. Thus this species lives on contrasting soil types in association with many different vegetational assemblages, from the coastal base to the crest of the range.

There is a rather wide variation in color in gambeli from the San Gabriels. Certain individuals taken in open, sandy coastal sage areas are pale, some being indistinguishable from examples of sonoriensis taken in the pinyon-juniper association on the desert slope. Specimens from San Antonio Canyon have somewhat darker pelage than those from the sage belt, and than individuals taken on Blue Ridge. Possibly a large series of Peromyscus maniculatus from the San Gabriel Mountains would show definite local trends in color of pelage.

This species is active on sub-freezing and rainy nights as evidenced by trapping results, and at Big Pines there were tracks around the bases of conifers after a heavy snowfall in December, 1951. Several females taken in the sage belt in October, 1948, carried embryos, and a lactating female was recorded from Blue Ridge on November 13, 1951. Juveniles have been taken in September, October, November, and December.

Specimens examined.--Total, 9, distributed as follows: Los Angeles County: 1 mi. S and 2 mi. W Big Pines, 7400 ft., 3; 1 mi. S and 2 mi. E Big Pines, 8200 ft., 1; 4 mi. NE Claremont, 1900 ft., 2; San Antonio Wash, 1800 ft., 3 (PC).

=Peromyscus maniculatus sonoriensis= (Le Conte)

Deer Mouse

This subspecies is associated with contrasting types of soil and vegetation. It is seemingly absent from the upper pinyon-juniper sage flats and areas grown to chaparral, but is fairly common on the gravelly benches dotted with junipers, and in the washes issuing from the canyons on the desert slope. It is present in small numbers in the Joshua tree association.

In 1951 the numbers of sonoriensis were noticeably less than in 1948; probably this was correlated with the series of dry winters in this period. In December, 1948, this animal was one of the most common rodents in Mescal Wash, 200 trap-nights yielding thirteen specimens; but in November, 1951, none was taken. In parts of the juniper belt, where an average of about six sonoriensis was taken per 100 trap-nights in 1948, the average had dropped to one per 100 trap-nights in 1951.

Specimens of this species from the desert slope of the mountains have been assigned to the subspecies sonoriensis. Those from Blue Ridge tend toward sonoriensis in color, and may be considered as intergrades between this subspecies and gambeli.

This species was active on nights when the temperature was as low as 10 deg. F., and individuals were trapped in the juniper belt in December, 1948, when four inches of snow lay on the ground.

Gray-pelaged juveniles were taken on the desert slope in December, 1948, and a female taken in Mescal Canyon on December 22 of this year carried four embryos near term.

Specimens examined.--Total, 11, distributed as follows: Los Angeles County:

8 mi. E and 4 mi. S Llano, 4000 ft., 6 (4 PC); Mescal Canyon, 4800 ft., 5.

=Peromyscus boylii rowleyi= (J. A. Allen)

Brush Mouse

The main range of this mouse in the San Gabriel Mountains lies between 1600 and 6000 feet elevation on the Pacific slope of the Mountains, thus encompassing much of the chaparral and oak woodland associations. It was the most common mammal in the oak woodland association in the lower foothills and often was trapped there on leaf mold beneath the oaks. While trapping for shrews I regularly took this species in riparian growth right down to the edge of the water. In San Antonio Canyon many boylii were trapped beneath logs and dense vegetation, and on wet seepage slopes adjacent to the creek.

This species shows a definite predilection for rocky habitats where these occur in the chaparral. In heavy lilac brush near Camp Baldy Peromyscus boylii was outnumbered by P. californicus, yet where talus slopes or boulder piles occurred boylii was more numerous. At the head of Cow Canyon amid boulders beneath scrub oak, bay, and big cone-spruce, this species was especially abundant and no other Peromyscus was taken.

Of special interest is the occurrence of this mouse on the desert slope of the mountains; there it was taken beneath scrub oaks in the pinyon-juniper association at the mouth of Mescal Canyon, and amid boulder and debris piles in Mescal Wash at 4000 feet elevation. While manzanita and scrub oak grew in the wash at the points of capture, the animals were actually surrounded by the desert conditions of the Joshua woodland, and associated with such desert forms as Onychomys torridus pulcher and Peromyscus eremicus eremicus.

Immature individuals were taken in October, November, February, and March, and a female with two large embryos was taken near Icehouse Canyon on November 8, 1951.

Specimens examined.--Total, 8, distributed as follows: Los Angeles County: Mescal Wash, 4000 ft., 1; Mescal Canyon, 4800 ft., 2; San Antonio Canyon, 5200 ft., 2; San Antonio Canyon, 4500 ft., 1; San Antonio Canyon, 2800 ft., 1; Thompson Canyon, 1800 ft., 1 (PC).

=Peromyscus truei montipinoris= Elliot

Pinon Mouse

Only once was this mouse found outside the pinyon-juniper association of the desert slope; in November, 1949, several were collected near Cajon in mixed manzanita, scrub oak, and greasewood chaparral. This was the only Peromyscus of regular occurrence in the pinyon-juniper area, and was recorded from the upper limit of this association, near Jackson Lake, at 6000 feet, to the lower limit of the association at the mouth of Graham Canyon at roughly 4000 feet elevation.

Although in the juniper belt truei often occurs on common ground with Peromyscus maniculatus sonoriensis, the habitat preferences of these animals are generally complementary. Where the mice occur together, traps set in a variety of locations caught Peromyscus maniculatus, but typically traps set amid the brush or on the open ground away from the junipers were productive. On the contrary truei was invariably trapped quite near the junipers and often in association with the large nests of Neotoma fuscipes simplex. In fact traps set right on the beds of litter beneath the junipers were most likely to catch truei. Records kept of trapping localities show that truei was without exception trapped within twenty feet of some treelike shelter such as junipers, pinyons, Joshua tree or scrub oaks. Thus Peromyscus maniculatus occupies the open stretches between the trees, while truei inhabits the ground beneath and immediately adjacent to the trees. In Nevada the pinon mouse prefers rocky areas (Hall, 1946:520). In the San Gabriel Mountains this mouse does not seem to have this predilection.

In the juniper belt truei was second to Dipodomys panamintinus in point of numbers. In the course of 500 trap-nights in the juniper belt twenty-two truei were taken with thirty-six Dipodomys.

I consider my series of Peromyscus truei from the desert slope of the San Gabriels to represent the subspecies montipinoris. The series is closely comparable to specimens of the subspecies montipinoris in the California Museum of Vertebrate Zoology from the Mount Pinos area, but differs from specimens of the race chlorus from the San Bernardino Mountains in certain diagnostic characteristics. In his recent paper on Peromyscus truei, Hoffmeister (1951) considered the populations of this species in the San Gabriels to be of the race chlorus. Hoffmeister had only one specimen available from the San Gabriel Mountains (Lytle Creek, on the Pacific slope) which was intermediate between montipinoris and chlorus, but on the basis of cranial measurements it was referred to the race chlorus. Specimens of Peromyscus truei from the eastern end of the desert slope of the San Gabriel Mountains and the Cajon Pass area would probably demonstrate that the race montipinoris, which occupies the desert slope of the San Gabriels, intergrades with the race chlorus, which occurs in the San Bernardino Range immediately to the east, in the Cajon Pass area. Although montipinoris occurs on the desert slope of the San Gabriels, chlorus may occur on the Pacific slope. I took no specimens of the pinon mouse on the Pacific slope of the San Gabriel Mountains.

In December, 1948, many small juveniles were taken in the juniper belt, and on October 15, 1951, two females trapped at the head of Grandview Canyon had embryos: one three and the other four. On November 13, 1951, a partially gray-pelaged subadult female was trapped which had recently suckled young.

Specimens examined.--Total, 17, all in Illinois Museum of Natural History, distributed as follows: Los Angeles County: Mescal Canyon, 4500 ft., 8 mi. SE Llano, 11; Mescal Canyon, 4300 ft., 2; 6 mi. SE Valyermo, 5100 ft., 1; Grandview Canyon, 6 mi. SE Valyermo, 5100 ft., 1. San Bernardino County: 1 mi. W Cajon, 3200 ft., 2.

=Onychomys torridus pulcher= Elliot

Southern Grasshopper Mouse

Grasshopper mice seemed to be partial to the more sandy parts of the Joshua tree flats where the mice were trapped regularly but not abundantly. This mouse inhabited the barren sandy channels of Mescal Wash but was rare on the adjacent juniper-clad benches. In the arid, sandy washes this typical desert rodent penetrated the high pinyon-juniper association.

Wherever grasshopper mice occurred they were outnumbered by most of the other rodent species. For example, on November 26, 1949, below Graham Canyon, 100 snap traps yielded 10 Dipodomys panamintinus mohavensis, 2 Dipodomys merriami merriami, 4 Peromyscus maniculatus sonoriensis, and 3 Onychomys torridus pulcher.

Where abandoned kangaroo rat burrows were common in the Joshua tree belt these burrows were used as retreats by Onychomys. Some traps set at the entrances to old burrows caught grasshopper mice.

Specimens examined.--Total, 7, distributed as follows: Los Angeles County: 8 mi. E and 3 mi. S Llano, 3500 ft., 1; Mescal Wash, 4200 ft., 5 (3 PC); 2 mi. S Valyermo, 4600 ft., 1 (PC).

=Neotoma lepida intermedia= Rhoads

Desert Woodrat

This species was on the Pacific face of the Mountains from 1600 feet elevation in the coastal sage belt, to 4800 feet elevation in open groves of big cone-spruce and scrub oak of the chaparral association.

The local distribution of this woodrat is determined by suitable nesting sites.

Although taken in different types of vegetation, lepida, without exception, was associated with rocky areas or areas supporting patches of prickly-pear cactus. In the channels of San Antonio Wash, lepida was commonly associated with jumbles of boulders and boulder-dotted cut banks. There the vegetation is sparse, and the rats dwell among the rocks; only their droppings and faint trails indicate their presence. Among boulders lepida builds only small houses of sticks and debris, and even these only occasionally. The effect of the prickly-pear cactus on the distribution of lepida in the sageland is striking; trap lines there yielded no woodrats where extensive rock piles and patches of prickly-pear were absent, but many rats were taken where patches of prickly-pear are plentiful. On an acre supporting coastal sagebrush at the mouth of San Antonio Canyon, at 1800 feet elevation, there were fourteen patches of prickly-pear, each covering at least thirty square feet. In these patches there were thirteen occupied woodrat nests. Only one patch lacked an occupied nest, and this one contained the remains of an old nest. On this acre there were at least thirteen individuals. In the sagebrush belt only an occasional large patch of cactus lacks a woodrat house occupied by lepida. Seemingly Neotoma fuscipes does not build houses in patches of prickly-pear.

Most of the houses built by Neotoma lepida are small and simple as compared to those of Neotoma fuscipes, and often in rocky areas no nests are in evidence. The most elaborate nests are built among the pads and spines of the prickly-pear and under laurel sumac or other large shrubs growing near washes. One of three houses examined at the mouth of San Antonio Canyon was on sandy ground in a patch of Opuntia measuring approximately 11 x 14 feet. The house was 14 inches high and 41 x 37 inches at the base. It was built around the main stem of the prickly-pear and a rock about 10 inches in diameter. The house was constructed of sticks of coastal sagebrush and buckwheat, and was dotted with dissected fruits and flowers of the prickly-pear. The main chamber was arched over by the main stem of the prickly-pear and was roughly 12 x 19 inches, inside dimensions, being reached through two three-inch openings, one on the east side of the chamber and one on the north side of the chamber. Two cup-shaped nests were inside the chamber, these being constructed mostly of grasses, and each resembling a well constructed bird nest 4 inches in diameter. The grass nests were free of feces, but feces were piled up against the west side of the chamber with many snail shells and dissected fruits and flowers of prickly-pear. Thirty-five inches from the main chamber was a third grass nest on the ground beneath a cluster of cactus pads. Next to this there was a blind burrow about eight inches long, and one and three-quarters inches in diameter. No burrow led to the main chamber, in this or in either of the other houses, but all had at least one short blind burrow beneath the house.

At many houses there were one to three grass nests outside the house on the ground, within four feet of the house. From each nest a well worn path lead to the house. Traps set in these nests invariably caught woodrats.

The many prickly-pear fruits and snail shells in and around the houses of lepida probably were remnants of food. So many of the rodents caught in traps near woodrat nests were partly eaten--usually the brains were taken--that I suspect the woodrats of eating their relatives. The heads of many composite annuals were piled near woodrat nests.

Immature individuals were taken in September, October, and early November, and on September 26, 1951, a lactating female was trapped near Palmer Canyon.

An old female bobcat trapped in Thompson Canyon had masses of cactus thorns beneath her skin, especially about the forelegs. These thorns were probably received while she was foraging in growths of prickly-pear for woodrats. The other bobcats from San Antonio Wash also had accumulations of thorns under the skin of the forelegs. Fragments of the skulls of Neotoma lepida were recovered from horned owl pellets and coyote feces.

Specimens examined.--Total, 7, distributed as follows: Los Angeles County: San Antonio Canyon, 4500 ft., 2; San Antonio Wash, 1800 ft., 5 (2 PC).

=Neotoma lepida lepida= Thomas

Desert Woodrat

These woodrats were present in rocky situations along the desert slope from the lower edge of the juniper belt down into the desert. Specimens were taken in piles of boulders in Mescal Wash, and amid rock outcroppings on the steep, barren, south slopes at the base of Grandview Canyon, whereas none was found on the juniper-clad benches.

This woodrat built no nests in rocky areas; however, in the Joshua tree belt N. l. lepida often built small nests at the bases of large standing or prostrate Joshua trees. There sticks from creosote bushes, along with cow dung and small stones were favorite building materials. Judging from the large number of unused woodrat nests in the Joshua tree flats it seemed that this rat was formerly far more common than it was in the period of this study.

Specimens examined.--Total, 9, distributed as follows: Los Angeles County: 6 mi. E and 1 mi. S Llano, 3500 ft., 4; Mescal Wash, 4200 ft., 5 (3PC).

=Neotoma fuscipes macrotis= Thomas

Dusky-footed Woodrat

This subspecies was widely distributed along the coastal slope of the mountains from the coastal sage belt, at roughly 1600 feet, up to 6500 feet at the lower edge of the yellow pine forest and was most common in the chaparral association.

In the coastal sage belt these woodrats are restricted to wash areas where large chaparral plants such as lemonadeberry and laurel sumac are used as nesting sites. In San Antonio Wash the occasional large juniper trees almost invariably harbor the nests of fuscipes. The general absence of suitable nesting sites in the sage belt probably limits the spread of fuscipes in this area.

In the upper part of the chaparral belt in talus these woodrats live beneath the angular boulders and build no visible houses. Several areas of talus occupied by woodrats were examined carefully and no sign of houses was noted.

Two juveniles were found in the stomach of a rattlesnake (Crotalus viridis helleri) killed in May, 1948, at the mouth of Evey Canyon. Remains of woodrats were found in feces of the coyote and gray fox.

Lactating females of this species were taken on March 16, and October 2, 1951.

Specimens examined.--Total, 4, distributed as follows: San Bernardino County: Icehouse Canyon, 5500 ft., 2. Los Angeles County: San Antonio Canyon, 2800 ft., 2.

=Neotoma fuscipes simplex= True

Dusky-footed Woodrat

These rats were recorded from the yellow pine forests on Blue Ridge, at 8100 feet, down to the lower edge of the juniper belt, at 3800 feet. Their presence there as elsewhere was determined by the occurrence of adequate cover. On Blue Ridge they were taken in and near patches of snowbrush, currant, and choke cherry, and one was taken beneath a pile of logs where no nest was in evidence.

The thickets of choke cherry in hollows on Blue Ridge were favored house-building sites of woodrats. Among the tangle of branches large nests were built, and in September, 1951, the remains of choke cherry fruit and gnawings on the limbs of these plants indicated that woodrats were active throughout these extensive patches of brush.

In the pinyon-juniper association most of the large plants were used as nesting sites, but scrub oak, seemed to be especially preferred. Because it often grew in a twisted irregular form with the foliage nearly reaching the ground, the oak offered good shelter for the woodrat nests. In an acre of scrub oak and mountain mahogany brush one-half mile north of Jackson Lake, at 6100 feet, thirteen occupied woodrat nests were found. In the juniper belt, houses were of more irregular occurrence, and were always beneath juniper trees, usually beneath the largest and most widely spreading individuals.

Those specimens from Blue Ridge, on the crest of the San Gabriels, are intergrades between the coastal race macrotis and simplex of the desert slope. Although specimens vary widely in color, comparison with series of these two subspecies in the California Museum of Vertebrate Zoology indicates that all specimens from the desert slope of the San Gabriels are referable to the race simplex. Two specimens of this species from the granite talus above the base of Icehouse Canyon at 5500 feet on the Pacific slope, grade strongly toward simplex. Hooper (1938:231) mentions that specimens of this species taken along the San Gabriel and San Bernardino ranges may be intermediate between simplex and macrotis.

At the head of Grandview Canyon, tracks indicated that a coyote had foraged for about one half mile along the edge of a tract of dense oak and pinyon growth. It seemed as if the animal had been foraging for woodrats. A gray fox trapped near Graham Canyon, in the juniper belt, had in its stomach the remains of a freshly killed adult woodrat. The remains of an adult woodrat were found in the stomach of a rattlesnake (Crotalus viridis helleri) obtained on the desert slope of the mountains.

Specimens examined.--Total, 6, distributed as follows: Los Angeles County: 6 mi. E Valyermo, 5600 ft., 1; 1 mi. E Big Pines, 6600 ft., 2; 1 mi. S and 3 mi. W Big Pines, 6000 ft., 1; 1 mi. S and 2 mi. E Big Pines, 8100 ft., 2.

=Microtus californicus sanctidiegi= R. Kellogg

California Meadow Mouse

Owing to the paucity of extensive areas of grassland in the San Gabriels, this is one of the least common rodents of the area. It inhabits, however, even small patches of grassland up to 4000 feet elevation on the Pacific slope, and is locally plentiful. For example, a small patch of grassland amid the chaparral at the mouth of Palmer Canyon supported many Microtus, and in San Antonio Canyon at about 3000 feet elevation meadow mice were found amid boulders and yuccas in a small grassy area near the stream.

Specimens examined.--Total, 3, distributed as follows: Los Angeles County: San Antonio Canyon, 2800 ft., 1; Palmer Canyon, 2100 ft., 1; 4 mi. N Claremont, 1800 ft., 1.

Family URSIDAE

−Ursus americanus californiensis= J. Miller

Black Bear

Eleven black bears were introduced into the San Gabriel Mountains "near Crystal Lake" in November 1933 from the Sierra Nevada (Burghduff, 1935:83). I do not know whether or not there have been subsequent introductions. There are still bears present in the higher parts of the mountains, especially north of the study area, where they seem to be maintaining their numbers. The grizzly bear that formerly occurred in the San Gabriel Mountains was exterminated there some years before the black bear was introduced.

Family PROCYONIDAE

=Bassariscus astutus octavus= Hall

Ring-tailed Cat

Large sections of the San Gabriel Mountains are uninhabited by this species, while locally, in the chaparral belt near water, ring-tails are common. Many reports of ring-tails were received from owners of cabins and homes who reside in the canyons at the Pacific base of the mountains. Because of the distinctive appearance of this animal it is likely that many of these reports were accurate. The reports testified to the presence of ring-tails in San Gabriel Canyon, Dalton Canyon, Palmer Canyon and San Antonio Canyon. Hall (1927:41) lists specimens from San Antonio Canyon. Kenneth Hill of Upland told me that ring-tailed cats often have been trapped above that town near citrus nurseries that are regularly irrigated. This species probably is not present on the desert slope of the range.

The only specimen that I took was a female weighing one pound and fourteen ounces. It was trapped on March 24, 1951, among granite boulders, beneath scrub oak and bay trees, near the mouth of Icehouse Canyon, at 5500 feet elevation.

=Procyon lotor psora= Gray

Raccoon

The raccoon was one of the most common carnivores in the San Gabriels and was found on both slopes of the range. Tracks were noted and one old male was trapped at the base of the Pacific slope foothills at 1900 feet elevation, and raccoons were captured at several localities from this point up to 5500 feet in San Antonio Canyon. They were noted on Blue Ridge at about 8000 feet elevation foraging around the camp grounds. On the desert slope they occurred down to the lower edge of the pinyon-juniper belt, for example near the mouth of Sheep Creek Canyon.

Sign of raccoons was most often found near water; tracks, however, indicated that these animals, along with other carnivores, used fire roads for traveling through the chaparral. In a small draw one-half mile east of the mouth of Thompson Canyon two raccoons were trapped although the only water was a series of small, disconnected seepage pools beneath the valley oaks.

A raccoon freed from a small steel trap in San Antonio Canyon concealed itself in an unusual but extremely effective manner. When released the coon splashed up the middle of the small creek nearby to a place where some dead alders had fallen over and shaded the water--here the animal squatted down in the stream. The raccoon was mostly submerged, its tail was floating, and its back and the top of its head and snout were above water. With most of its body under water, and with the maze of alder logs above casting a broken pattern of light and shade, it was well hidden. When closely pressed the raccoon hid in the same manner several times before it disappeared up a rocky draw into the scrub oak brush.

In the autumn of 1951, raccoons fed on grapes at the Sycamore Valley Ranch one mile south of Devore. The one specimen (P. C.) saved, an old male from 1/2 mi. W Palmer Canyon, had remains of beetles in its stomach and weighed slightly more than 13 pounds.

Family MUSTELIDAE

=Mustela frenata latirostra= Hall

Long-tailed Weasel

Several weasels were found dead on roads in the coastal sage belt near San Antonio and Lytle canyons.

=Taxidea taxus neglecta= Mearns

Badger

I found no sign of badgers on the Pacific slope of the range, but James Wolfort, employed by the state Fish and Game Commission to trap coyotes, reported that in 1948 he trapped also several badgers at the coastal foot of the range in the San Fernando Valley area which is west of the study area.

=Taxidea taxus berlandieri= Baird

Badger

Many old badger diggings were found in the Joshua tree woodland and pinyon-juniper associations of the desert slope, but none of the animals was observed nor were specimens secured. Mr. E. A. Eberle who has trapped for many winters in the vicinity of Mescal Canyon stated that he caught badgers occasionally.

I examined the skin of a badger taken at Llano which showed the characteristic paleness of the desert subspecies berlandieri.

=Mephitis mephitis holzneri= Mearns

Striped Skunk

The populations of striped skunks in the San Gabriels center around cultivated land at the Pacific foot of the range. Citrus groves, grape vineyards, and areas once cleared by man are preferred to coastal sagebrush flats. The cultivated areas now probably support many more skunks than were there under original conditions. I have many sight records of striped skunks which I obtained while driving through the citrus groves at night. Only once was the striped skunk noted in the chaparral; all the other records were from the coastal sagebrush belt.

In addition to insects and small mammals, grapes are eaten regularly by skunks in vineyards, and the fruit of the prickly-pear cactus is often eaten. Near the mouth of Thompson Canyon feces examined in October 1948, contained almost exclusively the remains of prickly-pear fruit.

A male taken one-half mile south of Devore weighed five pounds and four ounces.

Specimens examined, 2: San Bernardino County: 1/2 mi. S Devore, 2200 ft., 1. Los Angeles County: 3 mi. N Claremont, 1500 ft., 1 (PC).

=Spilogale gracilis microrhina= Hall

Spotted Skunk

Spotted skunks are common locally in the coastal sage scrub association and lower chaparral association on the coastal face of the mountains, mainly between 1000 and 4000 feet elevation; but they have been reported from Icehouse Canyon at 5000 feet, and I took one above the mouth of this canyon at 5500 feet elevation. A few spotted skunks may inhabit the lower desert slope of the mountains; here feces thought to be those of spotted skunks have been found, and a bobcat trapped near the head of Grandview Canyon smelled strongly of skunk.

The spotted skunk usually was in rocky habitats. In the sage flats, sign (mostly feces and tracks) usually was near rock piles and around human developments such as rock walls, old outbuildings and houses. Specimens taken in the chaparral were trapped near granite outcroppings.

In the autumn of 1950, at my house near the mouth of Palmer Canyon, a family of spotted skunks lived under the floors. Night after night they scratched under the floor and chattered in high-pitched rasping notes, and on several evenings one walked complacently into the living room. It finally became necessary to trap and deport most of these skunks. In all, nine skunks were trapped; these probably represented more than the original residents. One male was descented and allowed to remain. It spent most of the daylight hours asleep in an old shower room where the many gaps between the rock work and the boards allowed him entrance. Through no special efforts on our part he became tame enough to climb over us in order to get food left on the kitchen sink, and he would eat calmly while we sat only inches away from him.

Feces from sage areas contained mostly remains of insects and small rodents whereas many samples of feces from chaparral areas contained, in addition, shells of snails. Feces examined represent all months of the year.

Specimens examined.--Los Angeles County: mouth of San Antonio Canyon, 2 (PC).

Family CANIDAE

=Canis latrans ochropus= Eschscholtz

Coyote

Coyotes inhabit the sagebrush flats and foothills up to at least 4000 feet all along the Pacific base of the San Gabriels. This species seems most common at the foot of the range where large dry washes prevent man from occupying the land immediately adjacent to the foothills, and are the dominant carnivores of the coastal sage belt. Repeated observations have indicated that although many individuals range into the higher foothills they seldom are found deep in the major canyons or chaparral slopes. Coyotes rarely occur at 3000 or 4000 feet in San Antonio Canyon where it cuts into the realm of heavy chaparral; yet on steep foothill slopes and ridges, which are adjacent to the flat land, these animals range up to at least 4000 feet. Being hunters primarily of rather open land many coyotes go into the foothills only to find daytime refuge, traveling down dirt roads, ridges, and firebreaks, to forage at night in the sage flats. Coyote feces from the foothills, at about 3500 feet, contained predominantly the remains of such food items as cottontails, chickens, and jack rabbits. These animals could have been found only in the flats. This is additional evidence that coyotes do the major part of their hunting at the base of the range.

Observations of coyote tracks and trapping records have shown that these animals hunt mostly in the more open parts of the sage flats. Coyotes frequent areas of scattered brush, sandy areas, wash channels, and old roads, and seemingly shun dense brush. Many coyotes actually hunt for rabbits in the citrus groves near the foothills. On several evenings I traced their howling to orange groves, and Mr. Kenneth Hill of Upland told me of often seeing coyotes in his orange groves at night.

The forage beats of several coyotes were discovered in connection with trapping specimens of these animals. In January, 1952, two coyotes, probably a mated pair, traveled nightly from the slopes immediately west of Evey Canyon, at about 3100 feet, down into the sagebrush adjacent to the west side of San Antonio Wash, at about 1700 feet elevation. The route led down open ridges, then for about one half mile across a level, cultivated plateau, and then swung over the eroded banks near the lowermost point of the plateau onto the level sage flats. The distance covered by this route from the foothills down to the flats was somewhat more than a mile, with about a 1400 foot difference in elevation between the daytime retreat and the nocturnal forage area. Another route, seemingly used by only one coyote, was somewhat longer. This animal followed fire breaks and ridges from above Thompson Canyon down onto a fire road, and then into the lower end of Palmer Canyon where it entered the flats. This route covered about three miles in coming from the foothills to the flats. Feces of this coyote often contained the remains of white leghorn chickens which had been found at a refuse pile near several chicken ranches one-half mile from the base of Palmer Canyon.

Although no definite idea could be gained of the population density of coyotes in the area, it was clear that in certain localities they were, as carnivores go, abundant. After one large male was obtained in the flats at the base of Cobal Canyon, at least two other individuals were heard howling in this immediate area, and their tracks were noted repeatedly on dirt roads. One night early in January, 1952, immediately west of the head of San Antonio Wash, the voices of six coyotes could be picked out separately from a chorus of coyote howls which came from several different directions in the wash.

Many field examinations of coyote feces left the impression that chickens and lagomorphs made up the bulk of the coyote's food on the coastal slope. To check this a study of 39 sets of scats collected at various localities on the coastal slope was made in the laboratory, the results being shown in Table 10. Remains of one of the three species of rabbits, cottontails, jack rabbits, or brush rabbits, occurred in 72 per cent of the feces examined. Cottontails, it will be noted, were preyed upon more heavily than any other wild species, remains of this form being found in 33 per cent of the feces. The prevalence of chicken remains in coyote feces does not imply that these animals were killed by the coyotes. All of the chickens could have been found dead in the refuse piles of the many chicken ranches. In addition, the chickens were raised in wire cages above the ground where they were nearly invulnerable to predation. That coyotes may at times kill deer in this area was suggested by the finding of tracks in the sand in San Antonio Wash which clearly indicated that a deer had been closely pursued by a coyote. The tracks were lost in a stretch of brush so the outcome of the chase could not be determined. Near the mouth of Lytle Creek Canyon, in November, 1951, coyote feces contained mostly remains of grapes from nearby vineyards. Also, above Cucamonga, coyotes were found to be feeding heavily on grapes. This must be a rather unsuitable form of nourishment for coyotes, for many of the grapes in the feces appeared nearly unaltered despite their trip through the alimentary canal.

TABLE 10.--RESULTS OF EXAMINATIONS OF THIRTY-NINE SETS OF COYOTE FECES FROM THE PACIFIC SLOPE OF THE SAN GABRIEL MOUNTAINS. FECES WERE DEPOSITED IN AUTUMN AND WINTER (SEPTEMBER TO FEBRUARY).

Food item	Number of sets of feces which contained food item	Percentages of occurrence[A]
chicken	18	46.2
Sylvilagus audubonii	13	33.3
Lepus californicus	10	25.6
Sylvilagus bachmani	5	12.8
Odocoileus hemionus	5	12.8

```
------------------------------+-----------------+----------------- rodents (unidentified) |
5 | 12.8 -----------------------------------+-----------------+------------------ Dipodomys
agilis  |  4  |  10.3  --------------------------------+-----------------+------------------
Neotoma species | 3 | 7.7 ----------------------------------+-----------------+---------------
---- Mephitis mephitis | 3 | 7.7 ----------------------------------+-----------------+--------
---------- Carrion beetle | 2 | 5.1 ----------------------------------+-----------------+------
----------- passerine bird | 1 | 2.67 ----------------------------------+-----------------+---
--------------- bot fly larva | 1 | 2.67 ----------------------------------+-----------------+--
---------------- snail shell | 1 | 2.67 ----------------------------------+-----------------+----
-------------- scorpion | 1 | 2.67 ----------------------------------+-----------------+-------
----------- Jerusalem cricket | 1 | 2.67 ----------------------------------+-----------------
+------------------ sheep hair | 1 | 2.67 ----------------------------------+-----------------
+------------------ Lynx rufus | 1 | 2.67 ----------------------------------+-----------------
+------------------ Kitten of wildcat or housecat | 1 | 2.67 ---------------------------
--+-----------------+------------------ Lophortyx californica | 1 | 2.67 ----------------
--------------+-----------------+------------------ grapes | 1 | 2.67 ---------------------
--------+-----------------+------------------ grass | 1 | 2.67 ----------------------------
+-----------------+------------------
```

[Footnote A: This is an expression, in percentage, of the number of sets of feces which contained the particular food item out of the total of thirty-nine sets examined.]

The six coyotes taken on the Pacific slope are fairly uniform in coloration; the occurrence of white tipping on the tails of most of the specimens, instead of the usual solid black tip, is notable. Three skins, those of a male and two females, have patches of white hairs at the tips of the tails; two skins, of a male and a female, show only scattered white hairs at the tips of the tails; and the skin of one female has a solidly black-tipped tail. An additional female, trapped by David Leighton in Thompson Canyon, had a large patch of white hairs at the tip of the tail. Grinnell, Dixon, and Linsdale (1937:501) mention that only an occasional individual (female?) has a white-tipped tail.

Weights are available for four specimens: two coyotes trapped in San

Antonio Wash, a male and a female, weighed 20.5 and 23.2 pounds respectively; a female from the mouth of San Antonio Canyon weighed 21.6 pounds; and a large male from the mouth of Thompson Canyon weighed 29.3 pounds.

Specimens examined.--Total, 6, distributed as follows: Los Angeles County: Live Oak Canyon, 3000 ft., 1; mouth of San Antonio Canyon, 2000 ft., 1; 4 mi. N Claremont, 1600 ft., 2; 4 mi. NE Claremont, 1600 ft., 1; 3 mi. NE Claremont, 1600 ft., 1.

TABLE 11.--CRANIAL MEASUREMENTS OF CANIS LATRANS OCHROPUS FROM THE COASTAL SLOPE OF THE SAN GABRIEL MOUNTAINS.

==

================ | Four females | Two males | Averages Extremes | Averages Extremes ----------------------+-----------------------+-----------------------
- Condylobasal length | 180.67 174.2-183.3 | 188.35 179.2-197.5 ----------------
------+-----------------------+----------------------- Palatal length | 91.57 88.0-95.0 | 97.15 91.6-102.7 ----------------------+-----------------------+-----------------------
Zygomatic breadth | 90.15 88.9-92.0 | 95.60 88.8-102.5 ----------------------+----
--------------------+----------------------- Interorbital breadth | 29.12 27.9-29.9 | 31.45 28.1-34.8 ----------------------+-----------------------+-----------------------
Length of | | maxillary toothrow | 85.00 80.4-89.80 | 88.00 83.4-92.6 ------------
----------+-----------------------+----------------------- Length of | | upper carnassial | 18.30 17.8-19.0 | 18.70 18.1-19.3 ----------------------+-----------------------+----
----

=Canis latrans mearnsi= Merriam

Coyote

Coyotes are common on the desert slope of the San Gabriels below about

6000 feet elevation. They seem not, or only rarely, to penetrate the yellow pine forest belt, but tracks have been found occasionally near the lower edge of the forest, as at the head of Mescal Canyon. In the more open parts of the pinyon-juniper association, sign of coyotes was noted and they were the dominant carnivores in the juniper belt and Joshua tree woodland.

In the upper part of the pinyon-juniper association coyotes travel and forage in sage flats, along ridges, and in sandy draws, avoiding the extensive patches of scrub oak and mountain mahogany, and the steep, rocky, pinyon-covered slopes. It is apparent that the local ranges of the coyote and the gray fox in the pinyon-juniper belt are complementary, the gray fox keeping to the more thickly wooded or brushy parts of the area, and the coyote staying in the relatively open sections. Probably there is little competition for food there between these two canids.

As evidenced by tracks, coyotes commonly traveled and hunted along desert washes, probably because of the larger population of rodents and rabbits there. Below Graham Canyon three fairly recently inhabited dens of coyotes were found in the cutbanks at the edge of a dry wash in December of 1951. The cutbanks were six to ten feet high, and the dens were dug into the banks about three feet above the floor of the wash.

On the evening of October 20, 1948, near Desert Springs, Steven M. Jacobs and I set out a line of fifty wooden live traps for kangaroo rats. That night we slept about 300 yards from the middle of the line which was roughly three quarters of a mile long. When we tended the traps the next morning we found the tracks of a coyote over our own tracks of the previous day, and the first trap that had seemingly held a kangaroo rat was chewed and dragged for about fifty feet. Each trap that had held a rodent had been turned upside down so that the door had opened. At one point in the line where we had walked for about two hundred yards without setting a trap the coyote had followed every twist and turn of our trail. The animal had followed out the entire trap line and removed approximately eight rodents from the traps, reducing our take to one Dipodomys and one Peromyscus.

Examinations of feces showed that in the period from 1948 to 1952, while populations of jack rabbits were low in the Mojave Desert, the coyotes had fed extensively on smaller mammals such as kangaroo rats, and to some extent on fruit. By contrasting the present food habits of coyotes on the desert and coastal slopes of the mountains support is afforded for Errington's (1937:243) statement that predation is "a by-product of population." On the desert slope, with low populations of rabbits, the coyotes have turned to lesser species of prey; while on the Pacific slope, where populations of rabbits were high, the rabbits made up the major portion of the coyote's diet. On the desert slope, remains of the following food items were identified from coyote feces: kangaroo rats, mule deer, jack rabbits, passerine bird, manzanita and juniper fruit, beetles, grapes and apples. Near Valyermo, coyote feces were composed mostly of apples from nearby orchards. A female coyote killed below Grandview Canyon had its stomach and intestines stuffed with apples in large chunks. In the juniper belt, berries of juniper were often eaten by coyotes.

The three specimens of coyotes from the desert slope are clearly referable to the desert race C. l. mearnsi, both with regard to cranial and pelage characteristics. Although I collected no specimens from Cajon Pass or the passes at the west end of the range, it is in these places that intergradation might be expected to occur between the desert race C. l. mearnsi and the coastal and valley subspecies C. l. ochropus, as the higher parts of the San Gabriels seem to constitute a barrier to coyotes.

A subadult female coyote taken in the Joshua tree belt near Graham Canyon weighed 20.8 pounds.

Specimens examined.--Los Angeles County: 6 mi. E and 2 mi. S Llano, 3600 ft., 3 (2 PC).

=Vulpes macrotis arsipus= Elliot

Kit Fox

The kit fox barely enters the area under consideration. In the Joshua tree belt, below about 3500 feet elevation, tracks were most often noted in washes and on the adjacent sandy ground. The highest place where tracks were seen was a small sandy draw below the mouth of Graham Canyon at an altitude of roughly 3900 feet.

In the Joshua tree belt many old burrows were found but none was occupied. I believe these foxes are returning to this area where once they were common. In the winter of 1948 no sign of kit foxes was found, although intensive field work was done in the Joshua tree belt in the Mescal Canyon area. In December of 1951, in the same locality, sign was obvious and an individual was trapped below Grandview Canyon at 3500 feet elevation. Possibly since the use of poison for carnivores has been discontinued in this district the foxes are repopulating the area.

The one specimen taken, a sub-adult female, weighed two pounds and fourteen ounces.

Specimen examined.--Los Angeles Co.: 6 mi. E & 1 mi. S Llano, 3500 ft., 1.

=Urocyon cinereoargenteus californicus= Mearns

Gray Fox

The gray fox is widely distributed in the San Gabriel Mountains, occurring on both slopes of the range wherever extensive tracts of chaparral are present. They reach maximum abundance in the chaparral association of the coastal slope. Individuals have been observed occasionally at night in coastal sage areas at the Pacific foot of the mountains; however they seem to be less common here and probably come out of the adjacent chaparral to forage in the flats at night. Gray foxes occur all the way up the Pacific slope into the yellow pine woodland at 7500 feet, and from 6200 feet elevation on the desert slope down to the upper limit of the Joshua trees as, for example, near Mescal

Canyon at 4700 feet.

On the Pacific face of the mountains the gray fox probably is the dominant carnivore in terms of its effect on prey species, first, because of its abundance, and second, because of its forage habits. Some appreciation of the abundance of the gray fox may be gained from trapping records. On a fire road at the head of Thompson Canyon, at 2500 feet, two settings of traps about one-quarter mile apart were maintained for four nights. In this time four gray foxes were trapped. At the head of Cow Canyon, at 4500 feet, one trap set on a deer trail caught five gray foxes in five nights. At the end of this time fox tracks were noted about 100 yards away from the set, and another fox was trapped about one quarter mile away. In addition to their abundance, the forage habits of gray foxes are such as to bring them into most habitats present in the chaparral association. Tracks and feces indicate that foxes forage under dense brush, on open rocky ridges, in riparian growth, on talus slopes, and in groves of big cone-spruce and scrub oak.

Trapped foxes, if uninjured by the trap, were usually released. One fox was released on a small trail through thick vegetation consisting mainly of snowbrush. When freed, the fox whirled and darted through a patch of snowbrush for about seventy-five feet, then turned and disappeared beneath some large bay trees. Although the brush through which it ran was dense, the fox seemed to run at full speed. The success of gray foxes as predators in the chaparral is probably due in large measure to their agility amid dense cover.

The three specimens from the desert slope are referable to the coastal subspecies, U. c. californicus, rather than the desert subspecies, U. c. scottii. In all respects they resemble foxes taken on the Pacific slope; cranial measurements are near the maximum for the large U. c. californicus, and not small as would be expected if they were grading toward the smaller U. c. scottii. Floors of desert valleys north of the San Gabriel Mountains probably isolated foxes there from U. c. scottii found in the higher ranges of the Mojave Desert. Consequently one would expect no intergradation between the coastal and desert races in the San Gabriel Mountains.

An old female trapped on March 18,1951, in San Antonio Canyon, had three embryos each about 105 mm. long from rump to crown, and weighed 9.2 lbs. The average weight of four non-pregnant females was 6.8 lbs., whereas the average of six males was 7.5 lbs.

Specimens examined.--Total, 11, distributed as follows: Los Angeles County: Mescal Canyon, 4800 ft., 1; 4 mi. E Valyermo, 5200 ft., 2; Cow Canyon, 4500 ft., 2; San Antonio Canyon, 3000 ft., 1; Thompson Canyon, 2500 ft., 2 (PC); 1/2 mi. W Palmer Canyon, 2000 ft., 3 (PC).

Family FELIDAE

=Lynx rufus californicus= Mearns

Wildcat

Wildcats range over the whole of the San Gabriel Range, with the possible exception of the tops of the highest peaks such as Mt. San Antonio and Mt. Baden Powell. Sign of these animals has been observed, or specimens have been taken, from the coastal sage belt up to about 8500 feet in the yellow pine forests on Blue Ridge. The subspecies baileyi occurs on the desert slope of the range.

Wildcats are most common in the chaparral belt where they forage widely from the ridges down into the canyons. Judging from trapping records bobcats are not so common here as the gray fox.

Bobcats occur in the sage belt, where they are most common in the broken country around washes and in brushy areas. Although bobcats and coyotes occupy the same general areas here, the habitat preferences of these animals seem to be different, with coyotes occupying the more open country. An indication of the hunting habits of bobcats is furnished by the occurrence of masses of prickly-pear thorns beneath the skin of the legs, particularly the forelegs, of three specimens trapped in the sage belt. These thorns probably were acquired while the bobcats foraged for woodrats or cottontails in the patches of prickly-pear, which are locally abundant in the sage belt.

On March 12, 1951, a small subadult female bobcat, trapped at 4000 feet in San Antonio Canyon, was found dead in the trap and had numerous deep cuts around its head and shoulders, and severe bruises on the right shoulder. The spacing of the cuts, and the tracks around the set, indicated that while held in the trap this animal had fought with a second bobcat that had inflicted the fatal wounds. It seems unlikely that the fight was caused by a male attempting to copulate with the female held in the trap, for the female was found to be carrying an embryo.

In Live Oak Canyon, in December, 1950, tracks and bits of fur indicated that a bobcat had killed and eaten a gray squirrel. Remains of cottontails were found in the stomachs of two bobcats. All six bobcats from the Pacific slope had nematode worms in the pyloric end of the stomach.

Two females obtained on March 12 and 19, 1951, each had one embryo approximately one inch long (rump to crown).

The following list gives the weight of each of the specimens from the Pacific slope of the San Gabriels.

Specimens examined.--Total, 8, distributed as follows: Los Angeles County: San Antonio Canyon, 4000 ft., 1; San Antonio Canyon, 3200 ft., 1; 4 mi. N Claremont, 1900 ft., 2; Thompson Canyon, 1800 ft., 1; 3 mi. NE Claremont, 1700 ft., 2; Little Dalton Canyon, 1500 ft., 1 (PC).

TABLE 12.--WEIGHTS OF LYNX RUFUS CALIFORNICUS FROM THE SAN GABRIEL MOUNTAINS.

==

sex and age	locality	date	weight
[Female] ad.	3 mi. NE Claremont, 1700 ft.	January 20, 1951	18.8 lbs.
[Female] sad.	4 mi. N Claremont, 1900 ft.	March 9, 1951	12.5 "
[Male] ad.	Thompson Canyon, 1800 ft.	January 15, 1948	13.2 "
[Male] sad.	4 mi. N Claremont, 1900 ft.	January 26, 1951	11.3 "
[Male] ad.	3 mi. NE Claremont, 1700 ft.	January 27, 1951	13.8 "
[Male] sad.	San Antonio Canyon, 4000 ft.	March 12, 1951	7.9 "
[Male] sad.	San Antonio Canyon, 3200 ft.	March 17, 1951	11.2 "

=Lynx rufus baileyi= Merriam

Wildcat

This subspecies is widely distributed on the desert slope of the range, and was recorded down to the lower edge of the juniper belt. Tracks were observed on many occasions in yellow pine forest, but wildcats seemed to be commonest in the brushy parts of the pinyon-juniper association. Two were trapped in small draws lined with pinyons and scrub oak, and two at the base of rocky pinyon-covered slopes. Only occasionally were tracks noted in the lower part of the juniper belt. Bobcats are most numerous where woodrats also reach peak abundance, suggesting that woodrats are a major food.

The four specimens from the desert slope, although exhibiting a wide range of variation, are all representatives of the desert race baileyi. A yearling male from near the head of Grandview Canyon, at 5200 feet elevation, has the profuse black spotting of the subspecies californicus, but the general pallor dorsally is characteristic of the desert subspecies. An adult female, from 4700 feet elevation in Graham Canyon, shows the double mid-dorsal black line and the distinct black markings around the face characteristic of californicus, but is otherwise pale with reduced black patterns on the backs of the ears. The other two specimens, an adult male and a yearling female, are typical examples of baileyi, pale, and with reduced black markings. None of the specimens of bobcats from the coastal slope of the mountains showed characters approaching those of baileyi. It seems, therefore, that these two subspecies intergrade on the interior slope of the range.

A yearling male weighed 12 pounds, and a yearling female weighed 10.5 pounds. An old male weighed 19.6 pounds, and an adult female weighed 15.1 pounds.

Remains of deer were in two of the bobcat stomachs, and one of these stomachs also contained jack rabbit remains. Approximately a dozen nematodes (stomach worms) were in the stomach of one of the larger male specimens.

Specimens examined.--Total, 4, distributed as follows: Los Angeles County: Mescal Canyon, 4800 ft., 1; Graham Canyon, 4700 ft., 1; Grandview Canyon, 5200 ft., 2.

=Felis concolor californica= May

Mountain Lion

Several cabin owners near the mouth of Icehouse Canyon reported seeing a lion in that area in 1950, and others said they saw huge cat tracks in Icehouse Canyon. State Trapper James Wolfort reported that he trapped two lions on the coastal face of the range in 1947. Authentic reports indicate that mountain lions occur in remote sections on both slopes of the range, and in these areas mountain lions probably are as common as they ever were.

Family CERVIDAE

=Odocoileus hemionus californicus= (Caton)

Mule Deer

Mule deer are common in chaparral areas on both slopes of the San Gabriel Mountains. The animals or their tracks have been observed from the coastal sagebrush flats up to about 9200 feet on Mount San Antonio, and on the desert slope down to the lower limit of the juniper belt.

Deer are plentiful in the upper chaparral belt, and large bands are often noted there in spring. These bands may form in the up-mountain migration and reoccupation of areas which were covered by winter snows. A band of fourteen was observed on March 17, 1951, one mile east of the mouth of Cattle Canyon, and bands of about half a dozen individuals each were often noted in March, 1951, at the base of Icehouse Canyon. Cronemiller and Bartholomew (1950) gave a good account of the mule deer in the chaparral belt of the San Gabriel Mountains.

On Blue Ridge in the fall of 1951, deer were plentiful, usually being observed near patches of snowbrush and sage. They were seldom found in the coniferous forests. On November 6, 1951, while tending a line of snap traps before sunup, I startled a deer from its bed at one edge of a several-acre patch of snowbrush. In synchrony with the noise made by this deer's rising five other deer in various parts of the brush patch leaped up and made off. When bedded down in these extensive brush tracts deer are probably safe from an undetected approach, for a noiseless approach through the brush is impossible.

Two deer skulls from the San Gabriels were examined: that of an adult male from Evey Canyon, and that of an adult female from the mouth of Palmer Canyon. Using as a basis for comparison the cranial measurements for the subspecies californicus and fuliginatus given by Cowan (1933:326), these skulls were subspecies californicus. In none of the cranial characteristics considered did they tend toward the southern race fuliginatus. A young adult male, however, which was killed by a car near Cajon Pass on October 2, 1951, showed pelage characteristics of fuliginatus. Its fresh winter pelage was dark, and had the distinct black mid-dorsal line and the broad dorsal line on the tail mentioned by Cowan (ibid.) as distinguishing marks of the race fuliginatus. Its cranial measurements were not taken. Judging from this limited material the deer in the central part of the range, that is to say, in the San Antonio Canyon region, are of the race californicus, while fuliginatus may penetrate the extreme eastern end of the range.

Deer hair and bones were often found in coyote feces from the sagebrush belt. Some of these records may represent deer eaten as carrion. On February 6, 1952, tracks across a sandy channel in San Antonio Wash demonstrated that a deer had been closely pursued by a coyote. The deer had leaped from a cutbank onto the sand, had whirled around in several sharp turns, and had run into the adjacent brush. The tracks of a running coyote followed every twist of the deer's trail. The trail was followed into the brush where it was lost. Two bobcats trapped near Graham Canyon on the desert slope had hair and bones of deer in their stomachs.

Specimens examined, 2: Los Angeles County: Evey Canyon, 2100 ft., 1 (PC); Palmer Canyon, 1900 ft., 1 (PC).

Family BOVIDAE

=Ovis canadensis nelsoni= Merriam

Bighorn

Bands of bighorn sheep occur on some of the higher and more rugged peaks of the San Gabriel Mountains. Although I never sighted the animals themselves, I have seen abundant signs of their presence on the ridge sloping west from Telegraph Peak at about 9000 feet elevation. Several bands reportedly range in the head of San Antonio Canyon, and to the south on Telegraph, Ontario, and Cucamonga peaks. The sheep usually stay in the higher sections of the range, generally above about 7000 feet elevation. According to district Ranger A. Lewis some bighorns summer in the lower

East Fork of San Gabriel Canyon. The subspecific status of the bighorns in the San Gabriel Mountains has not been definitely determined. Following Grinnell (1933:211) they are here referred to nelsoni. If the band can be preserved without introduction of "alien" stock, the United States Forest Service and the California Fish and Game Commission will have registered an achievement that will be applauded by all persons who are interested in American wildlife.

www.ingramcontent.com/pod-product-compliance
Lightning Source LLC
Chambersburg PA
CBHW062016280526
45787CB00005B/2124